KU-092-364

Tbo
1978

Overcoming Common Problems

EDITOR'S PREFACE

The books in this series have been written to give help on a wide range of emotional problems which we encounter in everyday living.

The aim of the series is two-fold. First, to convey what is known and what is still not known, in a balanced and realistic way. Secondly, to show what help and relief can be hoped for and how problems can be better understood and made easier to live with. Each book has been written in a simple and direct style by a doctor with special knowledge in the field. It is hoped that the series will help the reader to realize that many other people have similar difficulties and as a result feel less isolated.

The first books in the series deal with hypochondria, sex, feelings about childbirth, and insomnia. It is intended to build up a comprehensive series covering a number of themes relating to common problems of modern life with the emphasis on practical help and guidance both to the sufferer and to those close to him or her.

DR ALAN KERR

SEX

Overcoming Common Problems

Other books in the same series

HYPOCHONDRIA
Dr F. E. Kenyon

FEELINGS ABOUT CHILDBIRTH
Dr Brice Pitt

INSOMNIA
Dr Peter Tryer

In preparation

SHYNESS AND ANXIETY
Dr Phyllis Shaw

STRESS
Dr Peter Tyrer

MID-LIFE CRISIS
Dr Brice Pitt

Overcoming Common Problems

SEX

Dr F. E. Kenyon
F.R.C.P.(Ed), M.D., F.R.C.Psych.

SHELDON PRESS
LONDON

First published in Great Britain in 1978 by
Sheldon Press, Marylebone Road, London NW1 4DU

Copyright © F. E. Kenyon 1978

All rights reserved. No part of this book may be
reproduced or transmitted in any form or by any means,
electronic or mechanical, including photocopying, recording or by any information storage and retrieval system,
without permission in writing from the publisher.

Printed in Great Britain by
Richard Clay (The Chaucer Press) Ltd, Bungay, Suffolk

ISBN 0 85969 156 X

Contents

TO APHRODITE

Introduction

You're interested in sex then? And so you ought to be! It is a fascinating subject which touches all our lives. But hasn't it been done to death lately? Not another book telling you what you ought to be doing? Surely the race has survived for thousands of years without the 'sexperts'! After all it's purely instinctive; just a matter of doing what comes naturally?

There is some truth in all this, but what we are seeing today is the creation of a new kind of anxiety, which we can call performance anxiety. Both men and women are being made unnecessarily anxious about whether or not they are having enough sex, the right kind of sex and particularly all those blissful orgasms they keep reading about.

This book is an attempt to allay that anxiety and at the same time to clarify for you the basic issues in what can be a complicated and confusing subject. I will concentrate on our present-day sexual problems, with practical advice and enough background information to help you understand on what that advice is based.

Sex has always been an emotive topic, with moral, religious, legal, political, educational and medical aspects. It's not just a private matter of two people 'having it off'. There is, too, the recent increase in the commercial exploitation of sex and to some people a threatening and disquieting flood of pornography.

Even though we are supposed to be living in a very permissive age, with high educational standards, there is still a lot of ignorance about sexual matters, which in itself can cause embarrassment, misery and other un-desirable consequences like unwanted pregnancies and V.D. It is often difficult to admit your ignorance or you might even think you are well informed when you have really picked up a lot of wrong information.

Moral standards are partly dictated by our laws; it is debatable which should or does come first, a change in society's attitude or a change in the law. Recent examples are the Abortion Act 1967 and the Sexual Offences Act 1967. You might say we get the kind of laws we deserve because they are made by our own freely elected repre-sentatives. This is the political aspect.

Sexual activity not directly connected with pregnancy or marriage has long been frowned on and frequently punished. When traced back, our legal tradition is very heavily derived from Jewish and Christian sources, which in turn were male dominated, anti-sex and anti-women. This is reflected in our double standards.

For example in some countries up until very recently it was possible for a woman to be prosecuted for adultery but not the man. We encourage our sons but not our daughters to 'sow their wild oats'. Male homosexuals have been savagely punished while lesbians have been ignored.

In the following eleven chapters you will find infor-mation about pornography, sex education, the basic differences and similarities between the sexes as well as practical advice on contraception and abortion. Normal sexual development is fully outlined for both sexes including such topics as adolescence, masturbation, love, engagement, the honeymoon and marriage. Marital sexual difficulties are covered, as are problems arising over pregnancy and childbirth.

There is then a detailed account of the types and causes of unsuccessful sexual intercourse along with what is meant by being oversexed. The effects of the change of life and old age are also noted. There is a whole chapter on V.D. and related conditions, followed by chapters on homosexuality and deviant sexual behaviour.

The last chapter contains a critical look at what is available in the way of self-help including the various sex aids you see advertised. I have also given enough detailed examples for you to understand the general principles of modern medical and psychological approaches to the treatment of sexual problems.

I

Books About Sex and Sexy Books

The scientific study of sexual problems, by medically qualified men, didn't really get started until the nineteenth century and then it was almost exclusively German doctors who wrote on the subject. Some of their books, often based on very extreme cases of deviant sexual behaviour associated with mental illness, became quite notorious. Pirated and poorly translated versions appeared and were sold under the counter. Unfortunately, in this way, they were treated like pornography instead of serious scientific works.

In order to avoid prosecution, many passages were left in Latin. One such famous textbook (*Psychopathia Sexualis* by Krafft-Ebing) had to wait until 1965 before being published in a reputable, fully translated edition.

Ironically our first great English sexologist—Havelock Ellis (1859–1939)—soon met up with native prudery and hypocrisy. So much so that his great work on homosexuality had to be first published in German in Germany in 1896. Later on he had to go to America to get published his encyclopaedic studies in the psychology of sex.

The man who has had the greatest influence which is still relevant today, was again a foreigner writing in the German language. Sigmund Freud (1856–1939) was an Austrian Jew, a qualified doctor and the founder of psychoanalysis. Even though many of his original theories have had to be modified or even abandoned, his ideas on sexual development opened a whole new era. But even such a genius as Freud was a product of his own time and society. Unfortunately he had very little idea about women and female sexuality.

One of the first women to write about sex who was also a pioneer of birth control was Marie Stopes (1880–1958). She was not medically qualified but had a degree in botany. Written while she was still a virgin and as a direct consequence of her own sexual ignorance and disastrous first marriage which was never consummated, her book *Married Love* (1918) became one of the great bestsellers of the century. At the age of 37 she married for the second time and this marriage was successfully consummated. In 1923 she published her book on contraception, the first Manual on the subject, which also went into many editions.

If you think I go on too much about not being medically qualified, as if doctors were infallible and the source of all received truth on the subject, let me quote you an example to the contrary. A very famous and respected Victorian physician's 'medical' views on the sexuality of women held sway for a long time. He was William Acton (1814–75) whose most influential book went into six editions. This is a direct quotation from the fifth edition of 1871:

> I should say that the majority of women (happily for society) are not very much troubled with sexual feelings of any kind. What men are habitually, women are only exceptionally ... I am ready to maintain that there are many females who never feel any sexual excitement whatever ... As a general rule, a modest woman seldom desires any sexual gratification for herself. She submits to her husband's embraces, but principally to gratify him; and were it not for the desire of maternity, would far rather be relieved from his attentions....

Compare that with today's sex manual or average woman's magazine!

One of the first popular sex manuals did manage to redress the balance a little. It was written by a rather prim and proper Dutch gynaecologist by the name of T. H. Van de Velde (1873–1937) and was originally published in Dutch and German. It had the reassuringly safe title of *Ideal Marriage*. It was not translated into English until 1930 but has been in print ever since. The title itself shows how his language and presentation so well caught the mood of the times, so that he was able to put across what at that time was very 'risky' information.

To bring you up to date I will just mention three other people whose names are very familiar and constantly crop up in any discussion of sexual problems, although a lot of people are very vague about who they actually are. The first is Kinsey (A. C. Kinsey, 1894–1956), an American biologist who was so impressed by the lack of reliable information on human sexuality that he set up an Institute and a vast research organization to remedy this deficiency. A number of famous books, written in collaboration with others, soon followed, the most notable being *Sexual Behaviour in the Human Male* first published in 1948 and *Sexual Behaviour in the Human Female* in 1953. They are crammed with tables and statistics and really established for the first time just what a vast range there is in normal sexual behaviour. He also produced the Kinsey Rating Scales, much used in research, which highlight the fact that people are not sharply divided into heterosexuals and homosexuals but can be rated on a sliding scale with several grades and mixtures in between.

This work was carried a stage further by Masters and Johnson. William H. Masters (1915–) is an American gynaecologist who in 1954 at St Louis, established the Reproductive Biology Research Foundation. Virginia Johnson (1925–), a divorcee with two children, not medically qualified but with a background in psychology

3

and sociology, joined him as a professional associate in 1957 and eventually as Mrs Masters.

They established the physiology of sex by studying and photographing volunteers having orgasms. It's said that over a twelve year period they observed and recorded over 10,000 male and female orgasms. They certainly made 'looking' respectable! The fruits of this research were published in the book *Human Sexual Response* (1966). They continued their work on disorders of sexual function, organized a treatment programme and published their results in a second volume *Human Sexual Inadequacy* (1970).

Of course there have been books on sex since time immemorial. One of the oldest is the *Kamasutra*, an ancient Hindu sex manual (Kama means love) written by one Vatsyayana (*c.* A.D. 300) sometime during the first millennium. In Eastern cultures the education of the young was considered a religious duty. In old Japan and China 'pillow-books', consisting of coloured prints of erotic postures, were given to young brides.

The written word and pictures have been very important influences on our sexual attitudes. It is in any case so much easier to give someone a book rather than face the embarrassment of having to talk about it. This raises the whole question of sex education, who should do it, when and how?

So much depends on the manner of presentation. What to some is an earnest attempt at sex education to another is sheer pornography. Even the Bible has been held to be indecent. For instance the worthy Noah Webster, the founding father of the famous dictionaries, in 1833 began the task of censoring the Bible, even to the extent of deleting whole sentences.

Nature has played a dirty trick on us, in more ways than one, by making our sexual organs and functions so closely linked with excretion, itself such a shameful, filthy, secret subject. St Augustine so delicately reminds us of this by his observation, '*inter urinam et faeces nascimur*'—we are born between urine and faeces.

This is one reason why sex has come to be associated with dirt; don't we talk about 'dirty old men', itself a double insult, as if the old have no right to a sex life. We also talk about 'smutty' or dirty jokes, and indeed the popular language we use also associates the two. Language is very important in another respect. Some people's embarrassment in talking about sex, for instance to a doctor, is made worse by the fact that they don't know what words to use.

Now I know you know, and practically everyone from the age of 5 upwards knows the rude 'four letter' words, which you will note describe both sex and excretion. I am resisting the 'trendy' practice of using them here, not out of prudery, but because they are so tainted with anger, violence, dirt and 'swearing'. They are, in my opinion, best left as taboo words and not made so respectable that they cease entirely to shock because swearing serves a very useful purpose. It is a relatively harmless way of expressing aggression and violent impulses so that if this is removed, a more serious way of 'letting off steam' may have to be substituted.

The Oxford English Dictionary always omitted them, but has now included them in the new Dictionary Supplements. There is the story that when Samuel Johnson published his English Dictionary in 1755 he was asked by an American lady why he had not included the four letter words. To which he replied, 'so you've looked then?'

However you present sexual information somebody is going to be offended or take issue with you. With sex education for children you can't win. If the subject is ignored, that's bad—children will learn the wrong way from dirty

5

jokes and misinformation from other children. If you do try and teach them, you're putting ideas into their heads, stirring things up and possibly causing all sorts of difficulties. Shouldn't it be left to parents? But what if they are too embarrassed or unwilling to undertake the task?

As we shall see later in this book, it is important how you are brought up about sexual matters. Leaving it all to the biology teacher is really ducking the issue. There is more to sex than the birds and the bees. But also to leave it to the chaplain or other concerned person can give an equally biased view. There is no snappy answer and clearly different children need different approaches.

At best sex education should arise naturally and continuously, along with all other things children ask about, both in the home and at school. Questions should be answered there and then in the way most appropriate for that particular child.

I do not believe that sexual morality should be separated off from general morality. If you are brought up to trust and respect others, not to hurt or exploit them and to control your own immediate needs when appropriate, these basic principles will also apply to sexual relationships.

The mass media, particularly the cinema and television, tend to trivialize, commercialize and further taint sex with violence. Women are worshipped as sex objects and at the same time degraded; good for selling cars or anything else for that matter. This has led not only to a strident outcry from Women's Lib but also the beginnings of a puritan backlash as well. These clashes and conflicts also bring a fresh crop of sexual problems.

Another facet of this is the current debate on pornography. One problem is the lack of an agreed definition—much of it, like beauty, lies in the eyes of the beholder. There are several different theories about the alleged harmful effects of pornography, however defined.

First is the 'safety-valve' theory: that it provides a harmless but effective outlet for your sexual fantasies, which otherwise you might act on. Secondly it may provoke in you not sexual excitement but disgust, shock, shame and guilt and so put you off completely. A third view is that it puts ideas into your head and you may then be sorely tempted to try out some of the things you've read about. Incidentally against this argument, nobody seems to be worried about you trying out various crimes and murders after reading the most popular type of book of all—the crime thrillers.

The fourth theory is the one that our present Law is based on, namely that pornography tends to 'deprave and corrupt'. Unfortunately the Law does not give any comprehensive definition of what this means. If it means anything at all I would take it to imply that it would cause you to act in a manner contrary to your established moral principles. Single notorious examples (like the Moors Murders case) are frequently quoted to support this argument; that possessing books written about sadistic acts turns you into a sadistic murderer. There is no convincing evidence for this simple cause and effect theory. And people conveniently forget the opposite sort of example. A recent instance of this was the case of a world renowned, deeply committed Christian theologian, who also collected pornography.

A fifth theory is that reading pornography can be a liberating experience; it may be good for both an individual and society at large to occasionally be shocked, disgusted and outraged. Also for ideas, prejudices and taboos to be periodically called into question. It may also be of some use in helping people with sexual problems.

Finally there is the view that it's all a lot of fuss about nothing. If you keep calm and deprive it of the 'forbidden fruit' element and just treat it as being in rather poor taste, it will soon find its own level and cease to be a problem.

It is perhaps just worth noting, in conclusion, that pornography is still largely produced by men for other men and is essentially concerned, on a fantasy basis, with the dread, fear and envy of women. How much this is culturally based is hard to say but there does seem to be a genuine difference between the sexes, at least in the visual aspect, in what 'turns on' men and women. Can you imagine an excited group of women photographers crowding round a man in a jock strap in order to take 'erotic' pictures?

There is though, a modern movement afoot for women to take more interest in their own bodies, especially their genitals and to depict them in art and sculpture. Comparisons are drawn between the form of her genitals and flowers and other products of nature. This is not intended to be either erotic, pornographic or crudely symbolical, as in the much used theme of deflowering virgins and say plucking a rose. It is partly a reaction against the Freudian idea of all women suffering from 'penis envy'; the illogical idea that just because the male genitals are external and there for all to see, they are in some way superior.

However, in some respects anatomy is destiny, and the whole concept of the 'mystery' of women is derived from this. Unfortunately there is no mystery. It is really based on their hidden sexual organs and the fact that when they do finally take everything off there's nothing much to see! And certainly no obvious sign of sexual excitement like a large erect penis. Many women are ignorant of their own anatomy and are a 'mystery' to themselves. How many have ever got a mirror and really studied their own external genitalia, let alone another woman's. A group in

America is having some success by running all female groups, completely naked, inspecting each other's genitals and even learning how best to masturbate.

Perhaps the other aspect to the 'mystery' of women is their power to produce sexual arousal by doing absolutely nothing! To primitive man, to get an erection, when all that happens is that a woman walks past, is magic, and a mysterious power indeed.

To cope with women's many roles, there is a tendency to try and split off particular aspects into types; this was done very effectively in Greek and Roman mythology by having very different goddesses. 'Types' such as the pure unsullied virgin, the mother, the prostitute and so on were defined. The difficulty arises when a real woman has to be all of these rolled into one.

As we have seen in Victorian times, women were made to feel guilty if they enjoyed sex whereas now they are made to feel guilty if they don't. Attitudes are also reflected in fashions. Clothes have three main functions; to keep you warm and protect you from the elements, express rank and position, and accentuate sexual characteristics. Women's fashions, at least up until recently, were largely designed by men. To be free you had to have, quite literally, freedom of movement.

Another way round some of these difficulties is to minimize the differences between the sexes and a lot of our recent legislation is aimed at 'equality' and against biased 'sexist' views. The same goes for our clothes, at least in the young, with the trend towards a standard unisex uniform of sweater and jeans. But it is idle to pretend there aren't any differences, apart from the obvious genital ones.

Men are, on average, bigger and stronger than women. There are certain things that women can do which men will never be able to, like menstruate, give birth, suckle, have multiple orgasms and be capable of sex at any time.

Let us explore both the similarities and differences in a little more depth, so that we will be in a better position to understand things when they go wrong.

2

His and Hers

There's more to sex than meets the eye. All reproductive functions are ultimately controlled by the brain, with two main channels of command: one via the spinal cord and special parts of the nervous system to the genitals and the other by the 'master' gland or pituitary sending out chemical messengers or hormones into the bloodstream.

Our sexual feelings and behaviour are governed, amongst other things, by seven main factors which usually all work together in close harmony. When one or more becomes out of step with the others, sexual problems can arise. Both the similarities and the differences between the sexes are also very much bound up with these factors, which are:

1. The external genitalia
2. Primary sex organs or gonads
3. Internal accessory organs
4. Sex hormones
5. Sex chromosomes
6. Sex of assignment and rearing
7. Gender role and identity

Sometimes sexual characteristics are divided into primary and secondary. The secondary ones are those not directly concerned in reproduction like the beard and hair on a man's chest and a woman's breasts and fatty hips. Even penis and vagina can be considered secondary. The decisive or primary characters are the chromosomes, the sperm, ova and hormones.

11

The external genitalia in the male consists of the penis and scrotum. The penis is made up of three long cylinders of spongy erectile tissue, which becomes erect during sexual excitement due to engorgement with blood. There is no bone in the human penis. The enlarged end is called the glans (literally an acorn); it is the most sensitive part with the richest nerve supply and is partly covered by the foreskin. At the tip of the penis is the opening of the urethra, which runs through its whole length and through which both urine and seminal fluid pass. The scrotum is the bag which houses the two testicles, the left one usually hanging slightly lower than the right.

In the female the vulva consists of outer and inner lips, around the entrance to the vagina. There is some variation in size but no truth in the idea that a large mouth means a large vulva even though both have lips. The opening into the vagina is partially surrounded by the hymen or maidenhead. There must be an opening for the menstrual fluid to escape. The hymen varies in extent and toughness and can easily be broken or extended by riding, using the fingers or inserting a sanitary tampon. You cannot tell at a glance whether or not a girl is a virgin.

Above the vaginal opening is a much smaller, separate one for the urethra, which is connected to the urinary bladder. Above this is the clitoris. It is very small, about $\frac{1}{8}-\frac{1}{2}$ inch (0.3–1.3 cm) long and does not hang free. In structure, except that the urethra does not run through it, it's a 'mini-penis'. Its sole function—and here it is unique—is that of transmitting sexual pleasure; its actual size bears no relationship to this. It can be so small and tucked away that it does seem a bit of a mystery. It's interesting to note that there are well over a hundred vulgar and other popular names for the penis, but none for the clitoris. Yet it is vital for a woman's complete sexual enjoyment. Just above the clitoris is the mound, covered by pubic hair, called the mons veneris or mound of Venus (Fanny's hill?).

The primary sex organs or gonads are the testes in men and ovaries in women. The testes or testicles ('balls', 'stones', 'orchids') are about 4–5 cm in length and oval in shape; the epididymis is a tortuous canal folded in on itself which forms the first part of the exit direct from the testis. The word 'testis' literally means a 'witness' (to your virility) and in less inhibited days a man would swear an oath with a hand on his genitals; hence our words testament and testify. The Greek word is 'orchis', so that the operation for removing a testis is called orchidectomy; the flowers, orchids, probably got their name from the shape of their tubers.

The testes develop inside the abdomen but descend into the scrotum shortly before birth. Occasionally one or both get left behind or stuck on the way down. Sperm is made in the testes, a process which continues throughout life. But the right temperature is needed for this. It is too hot inside the abdomen so that is why the testes are held outside the body, in the scrotum, where it is cooler. A testis left behind inside the abdomen does not produce live sperm.

The two ovaries are about 3 cm long and are situated inside the abdomen on each side of the womb. They contain thousands of potential eggs (ova) which are already formed and present at birth. One egg is released each month (ovulation) throughout a woman's reproductive life (puberty to the menopause).

The internal accessory organs are derived from the same primitive structures in the embryo in both sexes but subsequently develop very differently. The most important in the male is the vas deferens. This is a longish tube which joins onto the epididymis and along which sperm travel on their journey from testis to urethra, before ejaculation. It is this tube which is cut (vasectomy) in the operation for sterilizing men. There is also a small pouch called a seminal vesicle in which some sperm are stored.

The male, but not the female, has a prostate gland. It is about the size of a chestnut, situated close to the bladder outlet and surrounds the junction of the urethra and vas. It adds some further fluid to the seminal fluid and can cause trouble in later life by growing bigger. In examining for this a doctor is able to feel it through the wall of the rectum by means of a finger.

In the female there is the womb or uterus (Greek hystera, hence hysterectomy for its removal and also 'hysteria'), which is a hollow thick-walled muscular organ situated in the pelvic cavity with the bladder in front and rectum behind. It is usually pear shaped and measures about 7.5 cm in length, 5 cm in breadth at its upper part and is about 2.5 cm thick. It comes to a point at the neck or cervix, which juts down into the vagina. It is from the cervix that smears are taken to check for early disease (cervical smear).

The upper two angles of the uterus are connected to the tubes (full name, fallopian tubes); the Greek for a tube is salpinx, so inflammation here is referred to as salpingitis. A tube ends in a sort of funnel very near the ovary, so that an egg can easily get into it.

Another way in which we are quite alike is in our sex hormones, as both sexes manufacture male and female hormones, under stimulation from yet other hormones coming from the pituitary gland at the base of the brain.

The various types and names of the sex hormones are very confusing. As a group they are called 'steroid' hormones and this refers to their basic chemical structure. They are related to other naturally occurring substances, like cholesterol, which is very much in the news nowadays from the dietary point of view.

In your body your own sex hormones are made in the ovaries, testes, adrenal glands (or suprarenals as they are 'supra' or situated just above the kidneys) and the placenta ('afterbirth'). Many of these hormones can now be reliably estimated in either your blood or urine. Some of them or ones very like them can also be made synthetically in the laboratory and then used in treatment.

There are three groups of sex hormones:

1. Androgens (literally—'to produce a man') of which one example is testosterone. Androgens are responsible for the level of sexual desire in both sexes and in man for the development of male secondary sex characteristics. They also stimulate growth of bone and can cause the body to retain nitrogen and water.

2. Oestrogens (literally—to produce oestrus, Greek for 'gadfly', to bring 'on heat') of which one example is ethinyloestradiol, a common component of contraceptive pills. In general oestrogens are responsible for female secondary sex characteristics, control of some of the changes in the menstrual cycle and the maintenance of pregnancy. They also tend to build up protein and cause retention of water. They seem to 'oppose' androgens and damp down libido.

3. Progestogens (literally—favouring gestation) of which one example is progesterone, which interestingly enough is chemically very similar to testosterone. They are necessary for other menstrual changes, mainly in the second half of the cycle, the development of the breasts and maintenance of pregnancy once fertilization has occurred.

One difference between the sexes, apart from actual

quantities produced, is that in the female, hormone levels tend to wax and wane in cycles, whereas in males there are only very minor fluctuations.

The sex chromosomes have only fairly recently been studied when new methods were discovered for showing them up under the microscope. They are the final arbiters of true sex. The chromosomes are the chief ways in which hereditary influences are passed on to the next generation and differ slightly but importantly in the two sexes. Both have the same overall number of 46, made up of 22 pairs of body chromosomes (autosomes) plus 2 sex chromosomes. These are alike in the female and designated XX, but unlike in the male XY.

Some sperm carry a Y chromosome and others only an X; if a Y-carrying one gets to the egg first and fertilization occurs, a boy will be born; if it's an X-carrying one it will be a girl. So you will see that it's the father who determines the sex of the child. If it were possible to somehow separate out these two sorts of sperm (many attempts have been made to do this both in animals and humans) then you could always choose the sex of your child (what an awful decision to have to make!).

So that the true sex of a person, whatever they may look like externally, can now be determined by testing cells taken from the mouth or the blood to show up the sex chromosomes. This is legally acceptable. However nothing in nature is that simple so that there are rare abnormalities where there is one sex chromosome missing, more than two or other mixtures.

Another interesting finding is that if a Y chromosome isn't present and androgens do not influence the growing brain of the embryo, the basic pattern resulting is female not neuter. So it seems that the female is the original prototype, with 'maleness' coming as a secondary imposition (Women's Lib please note!).

Two other terms need brief mention, as they tend to get confused. Hermaphrodite, if strictly used, should mean that you have both testis and ovary, but it is also used rather loosely for people who seem, anatomically, to be a bit of a mixture. Bisexual refers to the presence of masculine and feminine psychological attributes and attitudes in a single person. But it is sometimes also used to describe somebody who engages in both heterosexual and homosexual behaviour.

But at birth the sex of the baby is judged by the appearance of the external genitalia, this being crucial for everything else that happens to you afterwards. Different attitudes are immediately apparent by dressing the boy in blue and the girl in pink. So sex of assignment and rearing is of fundamental importance for future development. Occasionally it's difficult to tell the true sex at birth, but if you are brought up and treated like a girl (or a boy), then by and large you will feel and act like one.

For this, yet another term has been introduced, that of 'gender'—taken from grammar where there are three genders—as opposed to the more narrow use of 'sexual'. We now talk about 'gender role' and 'identity', which really means feeling and knowing that you belong to one sex. This is something that is learnt, so that early environmental influences are extremely important here.

Probably the critical time for establishing this is from about 18 months to 3 or 4 years old. Any attempt to change later on in life is fraught with difficulties. The characteristics which any particular society at any one time consider to be appropriate for one sex, e.g. clothes, how you walk, hair, interests, demeanour—are not firmly fixed but it is these sorts of things which a child learns to associate with being a man or a woman. The present craze seems to be a 'unisex' one with the blurring of traditional roles but no doubt this will change again.

Before discussing sex problems in detail, it is necessary to have some notion about normal sexual development. Freud startled a lot of people in his day by talking about infantile sexuality. Outraged Victorian parents thought he was casting aspersions on their sweet innocent children, who may have been tainted by original sin but how on earth could they be sexual?

Actually any unbiased observer can see for themselves. For example, male children are capable of having erections practically from the moment of birth. Infants explore their world by feeling with their hands, and this includes their own bodies. So that a boy will play with his penis and a girl feel her genitals. Sometimes it seems they are also capable of orgasm by masturbation; going red in the face, grunting and groaning and then seemingly being relieved and relaxed.

Some mothers (who has a nanny nowadays? although I have met the case of an au pair girl caught teaching her charges to masturbate) get very uptight about this and in the bad old days children's hands were tied up and other types of restraint employed. It may even extend to mother not washing and drying her children's genitals properly, for fear of stimulating them too much.

As children get older they start to explore other people's bodies—brother, sister or friend—and play 'doctor' games. This is quite normal and too much should not be made of it. Boys have an advantage here in that they can easily compare and contrast their genitals with other boys'; this is much more difficult for girls. We need not take the extreme view that Freud made popular, that girls feel inferior and incomplete without a penis, even fearing that they may have had one which has been cut off.

Other Freudian ideas should not be taken too literally either. Freud used 'sex' in a very general sense of obtaining pleasure from various regions of the body, and not just as equivalent to 'genital'. The sexual energy which became concentrated in these different bodily regions he called 'libido'. The child was supposed to pass through an orderly sequence of developmental stages, such as the oral and anal, before reaching the genital.

At around age 3-5 years the famous Oedipus Complex reared its ugly head. In the case of the boy this meant loving and desiring his mother and at the same time seeing his father as a hated rival who would castrate him as a punishment. In the girl the process was rather more complicated as she was already 'castrated' (i.e., had no penis) but nonetheless she desired her father and saw her mother as the hated rival. After all this had been settled the child was supposed to go into the 'latency period' when nothing much happened sexually, until puberty started.

Little of this theory has stood the test of time. However it's perfectly obvious that, at least at first, you tend to model yourself on your same sex parent and can get annoyed with interference from the other one. But how your parents treat each other and how they adapt to and exemplify their respective male and female roles, also has a great influence.

Also, of course, how they bring you up as regards sexual matters is vital too. Whether you all sleep naked in the same bed or are frightfully inhibited and always lock the bathroom door may not be as important as you think, except in very extreme cases. Again Freud used to make much of the supposed effect of witnessing the 'primal scene' i.e., parents having intercourse. But you must remember he founded his theories on middle-class Austrian Jews at the turn of the century and made the mistake of thinking his findings held for everybody and for all time.

Nor is it true that we all necessarily pass through a

homosexual stage. Boys between roughly age 9–12 may go through a 'hating girls' phase, will gang up together, play rough games and indulge in a lot of horse play. The most upsetting part, for the child, in being caught in any sort of sex play, can be the horrified over-reaction of parents. Intense friendships between girls, vowing life-long fidelity, holding hands, swopping secrets and such-like behaviour or being a 'tomboy', do not either signify inevitable lesbian tendencies.

Puberty is the next major landmark on the road to maturity. We are still not absolutely sure what triggers it off but it is very closely related to the pituitary and its hormones. The age range at which it occurs is wide, something like 9–16 years for girls and 11–18 for boys with the average age for girls being about 2 years earlier than for boys (in common law it's taken to be 14 for boys and 12 for girls).

Certain bodily changes occur, usually but not always in a particular order. In girls it is enlargement of the breasts, appearance of straight pigmented pubic hair, followed by a period of maximum growth. Next pubic hair becomes curly (the short and curlies!), the periods start and finally hair grows in the armpits. In boys the corresponding order of events is growth of the testes and penis, appearance of straight pigmented pubic hair, early voice changes ('breaking'), first seminal ejaculation. Next you get the growth of curly pubic hair, a period of maximum growth, hair in the armpits, marked voice changes and finally growth of the beard.

It did seem, at least up to quite recently, that the age of puberty (as measured by the menarche or age at starting menstruation in girls) was getting earlier and earlier. This now seems to have stopped. Unfortunately physical and emotional maturity don't always go hand in hand and this may cause problems.

20

The 'age of consent' (for a girl to have sexual intercourse and to marry with her parents' permission) has remained at 16 years. This hasn't always been so. In 1576 it was a misdemeanour to have intercourse with a girl under 12; in 1875 Parliament raised the age to 13 and in 1885 raised it again to 16. One reason for doing so at this time was to make it more difficult for young girls to drift into prostitution. In 1922 Parliament again considered the matter and made it even stricter in that it became no defence that the man believed the girl to be over 16 (except in the case of a man under the age of 24).

We next come to the turbulent years of adolescence, which is now supposed to be over at 18 and not 21. It is really an artificial time span, starting with the physical events of puberty but ending with what? Not simply by stopping growing but by the achievement of maturity. But what do we mean by this? Basically it's the ability to stand on your own two feet, cope independently with life, have a realistic appraisal of yourself (good and bad points), to match up ambition and achievement and to make a satisfactory sexual adjustment.

The strength of sexual feeling (libido) and sexual capabilities unfortunately reach their peaks at different ages in the two sexes. Boys at around age 18–21 are at their peak but women may not be until age 30 or even later. Yet our society frowns on such liaisons. In other countries (mentioning no names) it is much more acceptable for a young boy's sexual initiation to be by an older woman.

The commonest sexual outlet in the young is still by masturbation; this is perfectly normal and does no harm. It may even continue after marriage.

Sexual experience before marriage is still an emotive topic, with boys, but not girls, encouraged to have some. This is reflected in the latest survey on the subject in which it was found that eighty per cent of men and sixty-one per cent of women admitted to having had premarital intercourse. It was supposed to be every man's ambition to marry a virgin and in the days when this was so highly valued—quite literally when marriages were arranged as a business contract—there was the ritual of producing the bloodstained sheets after the 'first night' just to prove it.

That this 'deflowering' could be both messy and painful, and not a very good start to a loving relationship may have been one reason for the medieval development of the *'jus primae noctis'* (right of the first night) or *'droit de seigneur'* (lord's right). The lord of the manor had the right to spend the first night with the bride of any of his workers. This was in any case often threatened with the hope of getting payment of dues instead. The situation is delightfully and delicately portrayed in Mozart's opera *The Marriage of Figaro*.

Even though in some quarters a conventional Christian marriage is regarded as 'old hat' and 'living in sin' a laughable anachronism, marriage is still surprisingly popular. However so is divorce. It seems the younger you marry, particularly in your teens, the more likely it is to end in divorce. Also what is sometimes forgotten is the fact that we are all living longer, so that 'till death us do part' can mean a very long time indeed.

By 1975 (but bearing in mind the change in the law in 1971) there were 120,000 divorces in the year, which was 7,000 more than in the previous year. Most people who obtain a divorce do so in their late twenties; the commonest duration of marriage ending in divorce was four years. But more than a fifth of the marriages that ended in 1975 had lasted more than twenty years. The number of couples divorcing while they still had children under sixteen rose by eight per cent.

There is more to marriage than sex, but sexual problems do loom large in many break-ups either as primary causes or as symptoms of a more general incompatibility.

Sexual adjustment in later life, due to our longer life span, is becoming increasingly important. Not only is there the 'change of life'—often in more ways than one—but also possible loneliness and a gross imbalance of the sexes. For example there are over three million widows in the country but less than half that number of widowers. Another difference between the sexes is that fertility can be lifelong in men but ceases for women after 'the change'.

However recent surveys showed that the average age of men who stopped having sexual intercourse was 68, with a range of 49–90 years. It was 60 in women, with a high of 81, the difference being due to the age differential between spouses and the shorter lives of men.

3

How Not to Have It

Two out of three girls marrying under age 20 are pregnant on their wedding day and twenty-two per cent of all births to girls under 20 are illegitimate. Why should this be? One of the most important reasons is ignorance about conception and contraception.

About 10 million sperms per gram of testis are produced every day. While in the testis they are still immature and further maturation takes place in the epididymis over about ten days, and during contact with seminal plasma at ejaculation. The final modification which enables a sperm to penetrate the ovum occurs in the female genital tract. Of the 100 million or so sperms deposited during ejaculation only a few hundred reach the fallopian tube where fertilization occurs. However it only needs one to make you pregnant.

Once released, an egg (ovum) has a lifespan of 1–2 days. When it has been fertilized it implants itself on the inside lining of the womb, where it gradually grows into the embryo.

Contraceptive methods aim at putting some barrier between sperm and egg, so they don't meet, or by so altering conditions that they don't survive or finally, by stopping their production at source. Although abortion should not be regarded as a method of birth control, it will also be considered in this chapter.

There are a number of dangerous false beliefs about how not to get pregnant. For instance it's even possible to get pregnant before you start your first period (if ovulation has occurred) and also through 'heavy petting'

24

without full penetration. This can happen if seminal fluid is on the fingers which are then put into the vagina or if ejaculation occurs outside the vagina but near enough for sperm to enter.

You can get pregnant if you have intercourse standing up, at any stage of the menstrual cycle (including during menstruation), without having an orgasm, and after childbirth while still breast feeding. It does not help to dance after intercourse, douche yourself out or if seminal fluid trickles out of you.

Nor do you have to be promiscuous to get pregnant. In fact it's more often the good girl who does, one who is quite unprepared, determined it shouldn't happen to her—the sort of girl who wouldn't dream of going out with a packet of French Letters in her handbag or be on the pill. She may get swept off her feet on one occasion (it only needs to happen once) or perhaps an unscrupulous boyfriend gets her drunk.

Whose responsibility is it to use contraceptives? Surely it is up to both of you, even though there are male and female methods available. But there is no 100 per cent safe and reliable method of contraception; I've even come across pregnancy following 'sterilization'.

Apart from abstinence the most reliable method is the contraceptive or birth pill, hereafter called the pill. Actually there are about twenty or so slightly different pills on the market, so that if one doesn't suit you another can be tried. In my opinion the pill should be given only under medical supervision, at least initially, as doctors are the best people to check on your health, discuss with you the pros and cons, and advise you about possible risks. Ideally your blood pressure should be taken as well as a cervical smear.

If you are under 16, technically the doctor could be aiding and abetting an offence by prescribing the pill for you, made worse by not informing your parents. But most doctors would prefer to talk to you privately about this and not inform your parents if you object, rather than you coming along later wanting an abortion. Very occasionally the pill is prescribed for menstrual disorders and not as a contraceptive.

There are three basic types of pill:

1. Combined—a mixture of an oestrogen and a progestogen, usually taken as 1 daily for 21 days, starting on the 5th day of your period, followed by 7 tablet-free days.

2. Sequential—oestrogen daily from 5th–20th day and then oestrogen plus progestogen for the next 5–7 days. These are not out of favour.

3. Progestogen only ('mini-pill')—starting on 1st day of period with 1 daily without any break.

The pill's main action is to suppress the hormones from the pituitary whose normal function is to stimulate production of the female sex hormones, which in turn cause ovulation. Thus ovulation is prevented and the progestogen probably thickens the mucus in the cervix as well as making it more difficult for the sperm to get through, and alters the lining of the womb so that a fertilized egg would not implant and grow. In terms of efficiency (i.e., in preventing pregnancy) the combined pill is the best; but in some cases oestrogens may be medically inadvisable.

Because the more serious side-effects have been associated with oestrogens no contraceptive pill should contain more than 50 micrograms; safer still are the newest ones containing only 30. The mini-pill may be better for you if you are breast feeding or for older women when fertility is in any case reduced but side-effects likely to be greater.

In most surveys 70–80 per cent of women are satisfied with their pill, but a large number of side-effects have been described which may affect the minority. There is no evidence to suggest that any of the pills available can cause cancer, although the very long term effects, say taking them regularly for 30 years, are still unknown.

Some side-effects associated with oestrogens are thrombosis, jaundice, intolerance of contact lenses, breakthrough bleeding, headache, nausea, vomiting, vaginal discharge, swelling (fluid retention), painful breasts and leg pains.

Progestogens may cause acne, bloating, depression, dry vagina, hairiness and reduced libido.

The combined pill could cause high blood pressure, irregular bleeding, weight gain, no periods after stopping and coronary heart troubles.

However a lot depends on the actual dosage, your state of health, age, other habits like smoking, drinking and diet, previous history (e.g., of depression) and family history.

Some of the alleged side-effects may also be due either to a neurotic attitude towards the pill or deep-seated unrecognized opposition to taking it; for instance, a dislike of the messiness of seminal fluid or fears of promiscuity. Your male partner may also object for similarly unrecognized reasons, like it being a threat to male dominance or fear of not being able to meet possible increased sexual demands. There is also the fear of being cheated (i.e., the pill being stopped without his being told) or the fear of her being unfaithful.

For some, intercourse which is absolutely 'safe' loses part of its attraction; there may be a neurotic need to indulge in 'risk-taking' behaviour, or an insecure man must keep proving his virility by causing repeated pregnancies.

All sorts of other types of pill have been suggested, such as a 'morning after' one, once a month one or a weekend one. But none are as yet safe and effective. Long acting injections or some form of immunization (you might even be able to be immunized against your husband's sperm but not another man's) are future possibilities.

The discovery of a group of naturally occurring chemicals called prostaglandins, which can be used to induce an abortion, may yet prove to be useful either as a pill or as an intravaginal pessary. Finally, work continues on a pill for men; all the ones tried so far have caused serious side effects, such as loss of libido, or feminine changes such as breast enlargement.

Another method of contraception is to introduce a 'foreign body' into the uterus which, as well as destroying some of the sperm also stops the fertilized ovum implanting and growing. Such a device is called, for short, an I.U.D. (intra-uterine device) or I.U.C.D. (intra-uterine contraceptive device); popularly known as the 'loop' or 'coil'.

There are many different varieties including the recently introduced copper ones. They need to be inserted by a doctor; the best time for doing this is during menstruation as then the cervix is most open and you won't be pregnant. A thread hangs from the I.U.D. into the upper part of the vagina, which you can be taught to feel. The copper ones need to be replaced every 3 years.

An I.U.D. may cause some pain or bleeding, or light up an old infection. It does not cause cancer or damage the embryo if a pregnancy does result. There is a higher risk of pregnancy occurring in one of the tubes (ectopic pregnancy).

Caps and diaphragms are mechanical barriers which stop the sperm getting into the womb. They may be combined with a spermicide, that is a jelly or ointment which kills sperms. There are three main types:

a) the diaphragm or 'dutch cap'
b) the vault cap
c) the cervical cap

The dutch cap is the largest and easiest to fit (there are ten different sizes). It is made of thin rubber in the form of a dome, the rim of which contains a metal spring. Medical supervision is again necessary as correct fitting is essential. Don't borrow your friend's, it might not fit properly! A few women are allergic to the rubber but otherwise side-effects are rare. Its greatest disadvantage is its inconvenience; it can be an unwelcome interruption during love making.

Spermicides alone are unreliable. They are put into the vagina, some requiring a special applicator. There are four types:

a) foams
b) creams, pastes and jellies
c) tablets and suppositories
d) c-films in which a spermicide is incorporated into a soluble plastic film.

The rhythm method or 'safe-period' is the only method approved by the Roman Catholic Church, but unfortunately it is very unreliable as the time between menstruation and the next ovulation is highly irregular. You also need to be a good mathematician!

The egg can survive up to 3 days and the sperm up to 4 days. The first day of bleeding is taken as day one and the day before the next bleeding starts as the last day. The unsafe time in the cycle is taken to be between 11 and

18 days before the next period begins. At least a year is needed to work all this out because cycles are so variable in length. The first unsafe day is obtained by deducting 18 from the number of days in the shortest of the 12 cycles and the last unsafe day by deducting 11 from the number of days in the longest cycle. So now you know!

To try and further pinpoint the time of ovulation (when you want to avoid intercourse) there are two additional aids. Taking your temperature (in the mouth) first thing every morning and plotting it on a graph. Your temperature runs at a slightly lower level during the first half of the cycle and ovulation occurs just before or at the time your temperature shifts from low to high. Special 'ovulation' thermometers are necessary as the rise is a very small one. The 'safe period' would then be 72 hours after the initial rise in temperature until the next period begins. The second aid is by your doctor helping you to recognize changes in your cervical mucus; at ovulation time it tends to get thinner and can be pulled out in threads.

Still one of the most popular methods is the sheath or condom (French Letter, FL, 'rubber', Durex is the name of one particular make). They are readily available from chemists, barber's shops, vending machines and other sources. The principle is very simple. The man puts a sheath made of thin latex rubber over his erect penis before having intercourse. It then catches the seminal fluid during intercourse. It is thrown away after use although there are some thicker, washable ones available which can be re-used.

Although basically one size (they stretch) there are all sorts of makes available, either plain or teat-ended. Reliable makes carry the British Standard kite mark and also a date stamp, after which time they should not be used. They should not be tested in any way before use.

Contrary to popular myth they very seldom split or

develop holes in them. The main sources of failure are not putting one on early enough, as even before ejaculation a little fluid containing sperm can come out of the penis; coming off when withdrawing, and blowing off during ejaculation because air has not been expelled from the teat end before putting it on. The only medical problem may be a rash due to an allergy either to the rubber or the lubricant.

Then there is the method of withdrawal (coitus interruptus) or 'being careful'. The man withdraws his penis from inside the vagina just before he feels he's going to ejaculate. Again this is not a safe method and spoils a great deal of the enjoyment. It is said that one quarter of the women relying on it will be pregnant at the end of a year of regular intercourse.

Male continence or coitus reservatus is when the man learns to postpone his own orgasm and ejaculation by stopping just short, waiting a while and then continuing. A man called Noyes thought he'd invented the method in 1869 as part of his way of life when he founded a sect called the Perfectionists of Oneida Creek in America. Actually it had been known for very many years, in the East and elsewhere, under various other names like 'Karezza'. It is liked by women but it's not a safe method of contraception and requires very great self-control on the man's part.

Coitus saxonicus is a crude and painful method where the woman violently squeezes the base of the penis during ejaculation to try and cause a backward reflux into the bladder. It is not recommended. Nor are temporary methods of halting sperm production by heating up the testes, either by hot baths or by continuous wearing of a jock strap with disposable paper insulation, even though a 70 per cent reduced sperm count has sometimes been achieved.

31

Other sorts of intercourse have been recommended such as anal intercourse. It is alleged that this is frequently used as a method of birth control in Catholic countries. Many women object; they feel they are being used like an animal and that it's dirty. It can also be painful without sufficient lubrication and stretching of the anal sphincter first. Occasionally the man can get a urinary tract infection in this way, and also infect his partner if he puts his penis in her vagina again without first thoroughly washing it. Also it's perhaps worth pointing out that anal intercourse is still technically illegal in this country although prosecution is almost unheard of.

Other ways of avoiding pregnancy are by love making to orgasm in different ways. This can be by oral-genital means; called fellatio when the man puts his penis in a woman's mouth and cunnilingus when a man licks and kisses her genitals. The one danger in the latter is of actually blowing into the vagina; this has caused at least one death by means of an air embolism! When fellatio and cunnilingus are carried out simultaneously in the head to toe position, it is called soixante-neuf or the 69 position.

Women may worry whether or not they should swallow seminal fluid. In fact it contains no nasty germs and is harmless and, of course, you can't get pregnant this way. It's simply a matter of personal preference. Like any other fluid it can go down the 'wrong way' and cause temporary gagging and choking, and so can the penis if pushed too far down the throat. The penis may also get damaged on the woman's teeth.

For complete and permanent avoidance of pregnancy, some form of sterilization can be carried out. Even though you may have heard that some of these procedures are reversible, when planning this you should both regard it as being permanent. The written permission of both partners is usually obtained before operating. Either the female or the male can be sterilized but you should talk it over with your doctor first before making any decisions.

The oldest and best known method in the female is to cut and tie both the fallopian tubes. There are over a hundred different techniques for doing this; it is possible to have it done without leaving an abdominal scar and under a local anaesthetic, but the exact method should be discussed with your doctor and specialist (gynaecologist). If other conditions warrant it (e.g., very heavy and uncontrollable periods or some disease of the uterus) sterilization can be accomplished by hysterectomy (removal of the womb but not the ovaries) which does not bring on the change of life.

After your tubes have been cut or tied you continue to have your periods as usual although they may become a bit more painful or irregular for a time. There is no alteration in your hormones, no change in your sexual feelings except perhaps for the better when the fear of further pregnancies is removed. The failure rate for these operations is extremely low. Occasionally sterilization is combined with termination of pregnancy (abortion).

In the male sterilization is by vasectomy, cutting the vas on each side. It is a simple operation, taking about twenty minutes and can be done under a local anaesthetic on an out-patient basis. Two small incisions are made in the scrotum to gain access to the vas on each side. Apart from occasional bruising of the skin or the wound getting infected, there are no serious complications. They are now being done at the rate of about 10,000 a year.

It is not such a new operation as some people think. It was being done back in the 1920s under the name of Steinach's operation, for the purpose of rejuvenating older men! Freud himself had the operation in 1923, hoping it might also help him to overcome the cancer which had just started in his mouth. The theory was that the operation stimulated the testes to produce more sex hormones. I am afraid this theory has never been proved, so that the operation fell out of favour until it was revived for sterilization.

There can be psychological complications following vasectomy, particularly in men who were unsure of their masculinity to start with, or have been browbeaten into having the operation or think it's going to help an ailing marriage or cure various sex problems. It may also get confused with castration but it's quite different. There are no adverse effects on your hormones, no effects on sexual desire or ability to get an erection or ejaculate, nor is there any outward and visible effect on your looks or appearance, so people cannot tell you've had the operation. Because the sperm make up a relatively small proportion of the ejaculate (maximum about 10 per cent) there should be no noticeable difference in its volume.

But what happens to the sperm? They are still manufactured but are reabsorbed back into the body again by special scavenger cells 'eating them up' and then disappearing into the tissues and bloodstream. However this process can lead to the formation of anti-sperm antibodies, the very long term effects of which are still not clear.

It is important to realize that you are not safe immediately after the operation as sperm may still be present in the cut end of the vas and elsewhere. So that two sperm-free ejaculations are necessary before you can abandon other contraceptive precautions. Specimens of seminal fluid have to be examined under a microscope by a doctor.

It is the number of ejaculations after the operation which is more important than the actual time, in eliminating any remaining sperms. Usually it takes about 10–12 ejaculations to accomplish this and as most men will have this many in about 6 weeks, this is the sort of time you have to wait before having intercourse without precautions.

Because there can be psychological and other complications following both male and female sterilization it is important that you both be given an opportunity for full discussion; and don't be embarrassed to ask any questions you want, it's your body and your future.

The subject that raises the most hackles is that of abortion. Doctors tend to use this word for all the different ways a pregnancy can prematurely end, including what laymen call a miscarriage. This is unfortunate as to many people 'abortion' smacks of a sordid backstreet illegal affair. But perhaps the danger now is of abortion being taken too lightly, always being available if things 'go wrong'. This could even make people less careful about taking contraceptive precautions.

Under the present law, which is still the Abortion Act 1967, there are four main provisions for carrying it out. You have to be less than 28 weeks pregnant and it has to be shown that continuing the pregnancy would involve risk to your life or of injury to your mental or physical health or to that of any existing children, greater than if the pregnancy were terminated. Finally that there was a substantial risk of your producing a severely handicapped child.

The two doctors who have to sign the appropriate forms to say that one of these conditions applies in your case are also allowed to take into account both your present and future circumstances. This is the so-called 'social clause' which has been widely misunderstood; it is not just because you're unmarried, have nowhere to live or can't afford it, on their own, but in assessing the risks to your health doctors are allowed to take these circumstances into consideration.

There is an 'escape clause' for doctors and nurses to opt

out for reason of conscience or religion. If this is so, your doctor should tell you his position and refer you to a colleague who has no such objections.

The Act is 'permissive' i.e., abortion is permitted but not obligatory, under these conditions, which if done in 'good faith' will not be followed by prosecution. The Act does not say anything about being raped, being under age 16 or feeling like suicide.

Abortion is still a serious matter as even done by the best doctors in the best hospital things can go wrong. For example from the time the Act became law up to 1971 there were 45 deaths—averaging about 14 a year. Of course there is still an occasional death from childbirth as well. The further advanced the pregnancy the greater the risks; these rise appreciably after 12 weeks. And the later in pregnancy the abortion is done the more it resembles a 'mini-labour', which is far more upsetting, both physically and psychologically.

If tackled early enough abortions can be performed by 'vacuum aspiration'. This involves expanding the cervix and putting a tube inside the uterus, which is then attached to a suction pump. This sucks out the whole contents of the uterus. It is usually done under an anaesthetic and requires being in hospital for 48 hours. There are efforts now being made to do this on either an out-patient or day-patient basis.

One recent series was done on an out-patient basis and used local anaesthetic (on the cervix) only. The average time for the operation was six minutes. The patient was then given a hot drink, lay down for half an hour and was then discharged home. Twelve patients subsequently needed admission as the uterus had not been entirely emptied and ten patients needed antibiotics for pelvic pain and high temperature. One woman continued to bleed and needed a blood transfusion. All these women were otherwise physically fit and none had a pregnancy of more than 10 weeks' duration.

More recently there has arisen the notion of 'menstrual regulation', which means doing the aspiration operation already mentioned as soon after your missed period as possible but before it's technically possible to diagnose pregnancy. Pregnancy tests done within two weeks of the missed period do not give reliable results.

Before having an abortion you should be given the opportunity of talking over all the possible risks and alternatives with a sympathetic doctor or other trained person. Possible physical complications are the immediate ones from the operation and anaesthetic such as excessive bleeding, infection, perforation of the uterus. Longer term ones are more difficult to assess but could be difficulties in conceiving again when you want to, spontaneous abortions and premature births.

Psychological complications are rare in properly selected cases where adequate pre-abortion counselling is available. Short-term guilt feelings and minor depressive reactions occur in about 10–20 per cent of cases. Longer term and more serious reactions (again usually depressive) directly attributable to the operation in about 1–2 per cent.

Do not try to abort yourself, either by using knitting needles or other instruments, by drinking gin and having hot baths or by taking quinine, 'slippery elm' or any other 'backstreet' preparations. Falling downstairs, dancing or moving heavy objects don't work either. You could make yourself very ill and also not succeed but perhaps damage the embryo in the process, only adding further to your worries.

If possible avoid going to private practitioners or advertised clinics or advisory services unless you are sure they are above board. All private nursing homes have to be officially recognized by the Department of Health and there are several registered charities which will give you unbiased advice. But in the first instance see your own doctor and don't keep putting it off and go on kidding yourself you're not really pregnant or hope for a spontaneous miscarriage.

There is a great outcry now, mainly as a result of women's rights movements, for women to have control over their own bodies and future, with 'abortion on demand'. This in itself is a very aggressive phrase—would not 'abortion on request' be a better one! I will declare my own bias—I'm against it. You don't go along to your doctor with belly ache and 'demand' he take your appendix out. You may have the diagnosis wrong, or not understand the procedures involved. Or you may be really unsure, perhaps being coerced by others. Nor should the mother be left as the sole judge in her own cause against the interests of the child. Finally it turns the doctor into a rubber stamp or mere technician, and so denies him his medical and human rights.

A full contraceptive service, sometimes in collaboration with a local Family Planning Clinic, is available under the National Health Service. So is sterilization, abortion and all supporting services, including special psychiatric advice if necessary.

4

Bring on the Girls?

The climax of all sexual activity is the climax (orgasm or 'coming'). You can hardly open a women's magazine nowadays without seeing an article on the subject. A lot of recent research (notably by Masters and Johnson) has helped us to understand more about it. The basic bodily changes are the same in both sexes. Endless and unanswerable questions as to whether or not women experience more sexual pleasure than men will not be discussed.

Whatever sort of foreplay or stimulation initiates a woman's orgasm the response is the same. There are two fundamental phases—genital congestion caused by an increased blood flow, producing vaginal swelling and lubrication, followed by a phase of muscular contractions. In women there is no obvious external erection (except for the nipples in some), the arousal response being largely internal, although there is some wetness of the vulva.

The clitoris or 'pleasure organ' has a rich nerve supply, as opposed to the vagina, which hasn't. According to Freud there were two sorts of female orgasm, a rather more primitive one initiated by stimulation of the clitoris and the more 'mature' vaginal one. This is now known to be incorrect. All female orgasms are triggered by the clitoris and are expressed by vaginal contractions, so that both are part of the orgasm.

During sexual intercourse the clitoris is stimulated partly by the man's pubic hair and partly by being stretched by the rhythmic movements of the penis on its attachments to the vulva. Penis size makes little difference

39

to this. Too direct stimulation of the clitoris during fore-play, either by fingers or tongue, especially when natural lubrication is not very great, may be almost painful. More gentle, indirect stimulation near the clitoris and around the vulva may be preferred, at least initially. The vagina is sensitive to touch only near the entrance.

Orgasm itself is accompanied by contractions of the muscles surrounding the vagina and in the perineum (the area between the vulva and anus). The uterus itself may also contract but it is only when oestrogen levels are low, for example after the menopause, that these particular contractions may be felt, rather like menstrual cramps.

Special nerve endings in the clitoris, vaginal and perineal muscles send impulses up various nerves to the spinal cord and so on to the brain. The exquisite sensation of pleasure, which is the 'feeling' part of the orgasm is virtually indescribable and difficult to compare with other people's. Certain parts of the brain are especially concerned with sexual pleasure and can discharge minute electrical impulses which can be picked up on a special machine for recording 'brain waves' (an electroencephalograph or EEG). So that you almost literally give off sparks!

The whole body is involved in convulsive-like movements rather like a fit, but a very pleasant and non-dangerous one. After the orgasm, which typically lasts 6-10 seconds, there is a phase of resolution, when the genital organs return to their original state.

The whole process has been minutely described by Masters and Johnson under four headings: excitement, plateau, orgasm and resolution. Men sometimes wonder if their female partners really are experiencing orgasm or just pretending. What other signs are there that she is experiencing the full works?

Earlier on there may be erection of the nipples and

swelling of the breasts. Later there is sweating, dilation of the pupils, an agonized facial expression, involuntary cries and shouts, a pulse rate of 120–180 and a progressive loss of intellectual capacities. Also there will be involuntary pelvic thrusting movements, a certain amount of generalized muscle tightening and spasm, and rapid, irregular, gasping and breathing. There may finally be a flushing of the skin from the upper abdomen to the chest and breasts which looks rather like measles! The trouble is if you are having an orgasm yourself you won't be in a fit state to observe all this!

Some differences between male and female orgasm are that women are capable of having multiple orgasms, that is one after another in quick succession, whereas a man is not. This capacity is retained by a woman throughout her life. She is also more slowly aroused, and returns more slowly to her pre-aroused state, but has no sort of ejaculation. The female orgasm is much more vulnerable to inhibition, so that a very common sexual problem is some sort of 'frigidity', whereas men often 'come' too quickly and easily.

What actually 'turns you on' varies enormously but in order to have a full orgasm it is necessary to have the right sort of stimulation, a reasonable level of androgens, an intact nervous system, healthy muscles and genital organs. Few women can have an orgasm by means of fantasy only (although this can occur during erotic dreams) and do not seem to be as easily aroused as men are by visual stimulation e.g., erotic pictures. Occasionally a woman can bring about a self-induced orgasm by stimulating her nipples or by crossing her legs and wriggling about like a little girl with a full bladder.

It is unrealistic to expect absolute bliss every time; it is quite possible to enjoy intercourse without having an orgasm. On the other hand if left in a state of pelvic congestion, this can be physically uncomfortable and you can also feel sexually frustrated. Relief can then be obtained by further clitoral stimulation.

The ability to experience orgasm varies enormously from a rare minority of women who simply do not know what you're talking about and have never had anything remotely resembling sexual feelings in their lives, to another rare few who 'come' too embarrassingly quickly. It may take many years, sometimes not until you are over 30, before you experience orgasm. There is perhaps a slight tie-up here with age of puberty; if this was relatively late, say over age 16 and associated with rather under-developed secondary sex characteristics like pubic hair, then you may be equally late in reaching sexual 'maturity'.

Some women, especially the sort who are very tense, meticulous and uptight and who may have had a puri-tanical upbringing as well, may find it very difficult to let go and abandon themselves. They may well have been taught that sex is rather nasty, dirty and animal and not for 'nice' girls. The loss of control seems frightening (as it may do in other situations like getting drunk or having an anaesthetic). The very expression an 'abandoned woman' suggests it must be wrong! We are back again to upbringing, personality, early experiences as well as social and cultural pressures.

Other fears may centre around being 'too small', being 'penetrated' in a nasty painful sense, the man going up the wrong hole; letting go so much that she might urinate or defaecate and hating the idea of being literally 'pinned down'. The vagina is relatively small but it becomes lubricated and swells during sexual excitement and after all it's been designed to let a baby through which will always be considerably larger than any penis! More specific causes of painful intercourse will be described later. But again expectations—what you have been led to believe and expect—are so important. We have already seen how the Victorians looked on it but now the pendulum has swung too far in the opposite direction, with loud cries about women's rights. You are made to feel guilty and inadequate if you are not always getting wonderful orgasms with the further implication that you're being cheated. Of course it's always easier to say it's not your fault and blame it on men for being such chauvinistic pigs and lousy lovers.

So many sex manuals concentrate on before and during but say little about 'after'. This can lead to problems, simply because men very rapidly lose their sexual drive after intercourse and may just turn over and go to sleep, much to their partner's annoyance (but we do say will you *sleep* with me!). As a woman's desire wanes so much more slowly and she has the capacity for multiple orgasms she often likes some 'after-play' i.e., to be held, cuddled and kissed and to be told she's wonderful and is loved.

There is an old saying, going back to Galen (A.D. 130–200) which is frequently misquoted as 'all animals feel sad after coitus' but what he actually wrote (in Latin) was 'all animals, save the human female and the rooster, feel sad after intercourse'! There is little to support this as all sorts of feelings can be experienced. There is also the other tradition that men are emotionally and physically drained, that it's equivalent to a five mile run and so on. Is it not stated in the Bible (Proverbs 31.3)—'Give not thy strength unto women'. So much is this believed that intercourse may be banned the night before an important match or sporting event. Obviously a certain amount of energy is expended, but what a wonderful form of exercise, and far from being exhausted you can feel very invigorated. But again so much depends on your personality and expectations.

The whole 'romantic' atmosphere can very easily be

spoilt by a too brisk or mechanical approach or even a too fastidious one. For example worrying about seminal stains on the sheets, rushing off into the toilet for a wee and a wash or even a 'nice cup of tea'.

Just how sexy a woman feels, how she copes with this and expresses it and how she gets on with the opposite sex, is best considered by going back over her life and development. How secure she feels in being a woman (feminine role) will also relate to past events.

The first man in a woman's life is her father and the way their relationship develops can have a long-lasting effect. He may, of course, be absent but other 'father figures' (uncle, grandfather) can act as substitutes. Without having to accept the Freudian version it is true that many girls do pass through phases of strong emotional attachments tinged with sexuality. For instance the little girl who wants to marry her father; the young adolescent girl indulging in innocent flirtations with him, trying him out, sometimes wanting to shock.

On the other hand the first and most important woman in her life, on whom she has to model herself, is her mother. How secure or otherwise mother is in her feminine role can be transmitted to her daughter. Also how happy she is in her own sex life. Does the girl feel wanted and valued as a girl or was it made plain that she was a 'mistake' or a boy would have been preferred?

Then there is the problem of brothers and sisters and the rivalries between them; how they compete for the love and attention of their parents and whether, as is usually the case, sons and daughters are treated in very different ways.

An overprotective attitude is the commonest difference in bringing up a girl as opposed to a boy. If overdone this can result in a lot of frustration and anger being stored up which then 'boils over' in adolescence with prolonged rebellion. This protection can start very early on, and seems to imply that she is one of the 'weaker sex' and particularly vulnerable to all sorts of dangers, from rape to abduction. How she is dressed, taught to behave and what interests and hobbies are considered appropriate are soon made apparent. Even slight deviations from the expected 'norm' may be met with great consternation, for example, not being interested in dolls and preferring to kick a football around.

Unfortunately early sexual experiences may be taken too seriously by parents, even the usual sex play with other siblings or children. There are very few girls, for instance, who get through life without at least one experience of 'indecent exposure' whether from a relative or simply by walking in the local park. These early experiences do not have the terrible effects that many people imagine. It's the way they are handled that is important, and it's best to make the minimum of fuss.

How to give girls a reasonable sex education is difficult. It is easy to be negative by always harping on the fact that there are a lot of 'bad' men about; never speak to strange men or accept lifts and so on. A happy balance has to be struck, otherwise a girl will soon acquire the attitude that men are 'all alike' and only want 'one thing'.

She will need preparation, too, in what to expect in bodily development and especially about her periods. I have already outlined the normal adolescent changes, some of which can be extremely embarrassing to a sensitive girl. The general growth spurt, development of breasts and body hair, blushing, acne and emotional storms, are some of them. You may not realize that your body is frequently not quite symmetrical, so that quite normally one breast may be a little bigger than the other.

The social and commercial pressures are considerable.

The insecure adolescent girl will spend hours in the bathroom and in front of the mirror in the belief that as long as she looks pretty she will be more acceptable ('face-value' has a very literal meaning). Up to a point this is true although later she will realize that personality and behaviour can be even more important.

Smell now becomes significant and perfumes liberally used. There are some very interesting connections between smell and sex, as shown by recent animal work on substances called pheromones. These are chemical substances produced by one individual which affect the behaviour or functions of another. An example known to most of us is a bitch on heat. Mammalian pheromones are either derived from or closely related to the sex hormones. The sex behaviour of male monkeys is pheromonally disorganized when the females are given 'the pill' and a police dog can smell progesterone on an object briefly held by a pregnant woman.

Whether or not we produce pheromones which cause attraction or hostility is still being debated. It has been suggested that this might be one explanation for women living closely together having their periods at the same time.

The slightly 'fishy' odour of women's genitals may be connected with fish being important religious and sexual symbols. Attempts to disguise this odour, again aided and abetted by commercial interests, by the use of vaginal deodorants, have not been successful. This is a good thing as they are both unnecessary and unhealthy. This perhaps was the final stage in making a woman just another product from the supermarket—pre-wrapped, hygienically prepared, bland, safe, ready for eating and disposable!

Just how old is a girl, in our society, when she first realizes that she is a sex object? When she first comes home and tells her mother a workman whistled at her? What incidentally, does mother say to this? Lucky thing, wish it was me, or, you are just beginning to find out how dreadful men really are?

In whatever way her mother handles these early experiences our society is geared to perpetuate the view of woman as a sex object. It trivializes her into a plaything or 'pet'; think of all those animal terms—chatting up a bird, sex kitten (with 'pussy' as vulgar slang for female genitals) and so on. These attitudes are also embodied in our treatment of famous or notorious women, especially film and T.V. stars. Here again women are so often referred to as sex 'symbols', idols, goddesses or some such phrase, along with the idea that they are eternally youthful, marvellously sexual and everybody's 'dream' (fantasy) girl. They are paid huge sums of money to show off their bodies and maintain this image.

They become idolized by both sexes; men desire them and women desire to be like them. Men have all sorts of sexual fantasies about them. But fantasy and reality are very different.

Such women almost inevitably have unhappy personal lives, are frequently immature (physically, emotionally and sexually) and may well have hysterical features to their personality. They are truly sacrificed. Women, of course, do fall for male stars (e.g., Rudolph Valentino) but not to the same extent.

It's no wonder that Women's Lib have over-reacted to all this, protesting at 'beauty' contests, getting rid of bras, and demanding to be treated like a person, not a thing. If carried to extremes this sort of attitude can cause further problems between the sexes. Not only in the way men and women react to and treat each other in social situations but also in their actual sexual relationships.

If not prepared, a girl's first period can be a tremendous

47

shock and can start as early as age 9. Again how mother reacts both to her own periods and to her daughter's can be crucial. For instance if mother always has headaches, sickness, pains and retires to bed every month with the 'curse', what sort of impression will her daughter get?

Periods may start and then stop again for quite a long time. They can be associated with cramp-like pains, be irregular or very heavy. Periods are also easily influenced by emotional changes so that if you become very worried in case you might be pregnant, your periods may well stop due to the worry alone. The pill can help both to regulate periods and make them painless by suppressing ovulation. The prescription can be so worded by the doctor ('no pack, no literature, no NP') that neither the girl nor her mother need know it's a contraceptive! Irregular and persistently heavy or painful periods later on in life need thorough specialist investigation.

During the ten days or so before a period is due you may experience symptoms of what has been called pre-menstrual tension. Symptoms include irritability, moodi-ness, nervousness and forgetfulness along with headaches, tender breasts and some swelling of the body (e.g., wedding ring becomes very tight). Sexual desire may be at its height just before or just after a period. There are no medical reasons why you shouldn't have sexual intercourse during a period, although it may be a little messy. (This can be temporarily overcome by wearing a dutch cap.)

Because adolescent girls, but not boys, are all very weight conscious and constantly being advised about slimming, they may develop a condition of compulsive slimming or anorexia nervosa. When weight loss becomes extreme, periods stop and the condition can get so serious that expert psychiatric treatment is needed. Essentially what lies behind this is a profound immaturity; a fear of growing up, of getting 'fat' (i.e., pregnant), of facing up to adult sexuality and being independent. Starving and stopping your periods serves many functions; it makes you unattractive, stops any sexual feelings, makes you like a child again (i.e., pre-pubertal, no periods and can't conceive) and gets rid of the constant reminder (periods) that you are a woman.

Most parental arguments nowadays with adolescent girls centre around their clothes (especially shoes), make-up, boyfriends, drinking, drugs and late hours. However before this stage is reached many girls pass through a phase of being devoted to an animal, usually a horse or dog. This is in some respects a rehearsal of the maternal role—something she can love, cherish, feed and look after, but there is also a sexual element as well. An animal is not a 'threat' to her, she can easily feel superior and safe, as it makes no demands on her, either sexual or otherwise. But at the same time a certain amount of vicarious sexual stimulation can be obtained, for instance in riding. It has sometimes been rather crudely stated as 'girls ride, boys masturbate', but some girls do both!

It cannot be reiterated too frequently that masturbation is perfectly normal and harmless in girls as well as boys. The only possible danger to girls, apart from guilt feelings and wrong information that she'll harm her prospects, is from pushing objects into the vagina, be it banana or vibrator. This can sometimes lead to minor physical damage or introduce infection. Clitoral stimulation using fingers is much safer.

At this stage the girl is also reading a lot of 'romantic' stories and magazines. This again fosters the impression that as long as she looks right (it doesn't matter how she behaves or speaks) and preferably uses well advertised 'beauty' aides, then Prince Charming or Mr Right will automatically pop up and she will 'fall' in love and live happily ever after.

It is conveniently forgotten that romantic love was originally adulterous love and that marrying for 'love' is a relatively modern idea and not shared by all cultures even today. In olden times marriages were arranged as a social and financial transaction, to weld two families together, to gain more land or a valuable dowry.

How do you know you're in love? Is it only sexual attraction, 'calf love', infatuation or something else? Is he just saying it to get me to have sex? It is a very complicated emotion which I won't attempt to define but just point out several different types, all of which may be experienced when a man and a woman are 'truly' in love. This is shown by the use of such phrases as: 'I want you, I worship you, I need you, I want to be with you all the time, share everything with you and this is the greatest, most indescribable experience of my life'. Four kinds of love are:

1. Sex, lust or libido.
2. Eros—the drive to create or procreate, to achieve higher forms of being in a relationship.
3. Philia—friendship or brotherly love.
4. Agape—altruistic love, devoted to the welfare of others.

But let's come down to earth again to what used to be the old practical problem for the girl—how far shall I let him go? This problem seems now to have been transformed into the question, does he love me? If she can convince herself of this, then anything goes!

Actually the first sexual experience may be very disappointing. So much depends on the background factors already discussed as well as on the actual circumstances. It could be marred by guilt feelings of having 'given in' or of losing him 'once he's got what he wanted'. Or quite literally not knowing what to do, or being a big disappointment to him or finally feeling cheap and nasty. Fears of pregnancy or V.D. can be overcome by adequate advice and education.

A girl may in fact still have no real inclination for sex but be goaded on by friends, some of whom make up their 'conquests' or continually go on about being late with their periods to gain esteem and popularity. Or she may be under a different sort of pressure, to 'settle down' with constant reminders of the opposite danger of being 'left on the shelf'.

It is a paradox that in our society you are prized and highly respected for being a virgin as long as you don't stay that way too long! Also the use of 'virgin' applied almost exclusively to females. Single women—spinsters, maiden aunts and other older presumed virgins—are at best pitied, at most despised. But why shouldn't a woman pursue a career, remain single and have no sex life if that's what she wants or take a lover when she feels like it? These are people for whom sex is not important, and celibacy can be quite compatible with good health, both mental and physical.

But for the rather shy girl who does want a mate, either temporarily or permanently, although more difficult for her than a man similarly placed, there are ways and means of going about it.

You can join a club or some other organization with a common interest or purpose. You can advertise (under an anonymous box number) in a local paper or go to a marriage bureau. There are also special holidays arranged for single people. There may be social opportunities at work, or connected with a local church or youth organization. Girl friends may have brothers or 'ex' boy friends or might arrange a 'blind date'.

If you are really getting seriously worried about this, even depressed, feeling inadequate and inferior, and perhaps fear you might also be 'queer', then go and see your doctor who will arrange for you to see a psychiatrist or other trained person to help you sort yourself out.

5

Boys Will be Men

Little attention has been paid to the male orgasm; it usually comes (literally) only too easily with ejaculation. The main emphasis throughout male sexuality is on performance, with the ultimate aim being the ability to 'satisfy' a woman.

However the mechanisms involved in the sexual act in the male are very finely balanced and easily put out of gear. Sexual excitement is shown by the penis becoming erect—something very obvious for all to see—so there is no question of 'pretending'. Erection depends on the penis becoming engorged with blood, which in turn depends on certain involuntary nervous reflexes.

These are governed by a part of the nervous system called the autonomic because it is not normally under voluntary control. Part of this system, known as the parasympathetic, is responsible for erection and the nerve fibres come from the lower parts of the spinal cord. In fact the same nerve centres which supply similar nerves to the bladder and rectum.

The penis is rather like a hydraulic jack which is pumped up by fluid pressure, with blood being the fluid concerned. There are further nerve centres higher up in the spinal cord connected to the lower ones, which in turn connect up with the brain itself. These are also concerned with sexual response to touch, visual and mental stimuli. It is necessary for courtship and sexual intercourse for a man to have the ability to maintain an erection without ejaculating.

Ejaculation is controlled by the second division of the

53

autonomic system called the sympathetic. This in some respects works in opposite ways to the parasympathetic, although they can act in unison. The spinal centre for ejaculation is higher up than the one concerned with erection.

Initially there is some voluntary control until you get on to 'two stroke' when it becomes inevitable. There is then a contraction of the internal reproductive organs, vas, prostate, seminal vesicles and the internal part of the urethra. This is emission.

Once this has occurred it is difficult to contain the next phase, of ejaculation, when spurts of seminal fluid are forced out of the penis. The first three or four contractions are so powerful that during masturbation the fluid can be projected as far as 3–4 feet. It is caused by rhythmic contractions of the penile urethra and muscles of the penis base and perineum, giving 3–7 ejaculatory spurts at 0.8 second intervals. Ejaculation is accompanied by the feeling of intense pleasure of orgasm.

Following this, and unlike the female, there is a refractory period when further erection and ejaculation is impossible.

That ejaculation and orgasm are closely linked is shown by the fact that the pleasurable sensation is usually greater the greater the volume of ejaculate. So if you've not had an orgasm for some time, when you do, it feels really good. However on rare occasions the two can be separated, as in 'dry run' orgasm. The subjective sense of pleasure varies from man to man, and to a lesser degree from occasion to occasion in the same man.

Apart from the mechanics of the sex act, a happy and satisfactory sex life depends very much, as in the female, on upbringing and earlier experiences at critical phases of development. Again we do not need to take too literally the Freudian story of the Oedipus Complex. But of course relationships with his parents or their substitutes are vital for learning to be 'a man', whatever characteristics of this are considered normal by his own family and society at large.

How a boy models himself on his father depends, in part, on what sort of man his father really is, but even more so on how the boy sees him and reacts to him. A father may have very old-fashioned and rigid ideas about such things as discipline and showing your feelings (or more likely not showing them). His attitude towards the opposite sex is shown both by what he says and how he behaves towards his wife and other women. Some fathers get worried in case their boy gets too pampered, turns into a cissy and by implication (although seldom voiced like this) into a homosexual.

A mother can be too overprotective or too seductive and treat 'her' boy like a girl or sometimes almost like a substitute husband, particularly if her real husband is away a lot or they don't get on. In any case in most households, at least in his early years, a boy will see much more of his mother and she will be mainly responsible for such things as toilet training. This, along with eating, often become important 'battle grounds' for future character development. Also the way mother copes with infantile sexuality, early masturbation, spontaneous erections and personal hygiene can all influence later attitudes.

An early decision is sometimes made about circumcision (the removal of the foreskin), mistakenly early in some cases, before it's had time to develop properly and separate from the glans penis. There is only one common medical reason for doing it and that is for the condition of phimosis. This is when the foreskin is so tight that it is impossible to pull it back and constriction so great that even passing water may be difficult.

There is no convincing evidence that circumcision

makes a man either a better or a worse lover, nor, as was once thought, any less likely to cause cancer of the cervix in his female partner. By adolescence the foreskin should be fully retractable, to uncover the glans, so that the smegma (the white cheesy material that tends to accumulate underneath) can more easily be washed away.

Circumcision as a religious ritual is another matter. Those in doubt on this score should perhaps heed St Paul's sensible comment (I Corinthians 19) 'Circumcision or uncircumcision is neither here nor there; what matters is to keep God's commands'.

Although circumcision is traditionally associated with the removal of the male foreskin there is also an ancient tradition of operating on females as well. In this operation the clitoris and inner lips of the vulva were removed. In early Victorian days partial circumcision by removal of the clitoris was sometimes advised to stop girls masturbating. This is not to be confused with infibulation or sewing up the entrance to the vagina to maintain chastity sometimes done as a semi-religious rite in some tribes.

Boys certainly value their manhood (penis) from quite an early age and play games such as seeing who can project a stream of urine the farthest as well as comparing shape and size with each other. So right from the start a male's sexuality is very obvious and no mystery. Nevertheless he may find lack of control over erections very embarrassing, for instance when this happens travelling in a bus or train or when worried or generally excited. This may be increased by fears of having an 'accident' i.e., wetting himself, which can occur very easily when first indulging in necking and petting.

Also 'wet dreams' (nocturnal pollutions) can be a problem to both adolescents or older men without other sexual outlets. It is again something over which he has very little conscious control and does not mean he's a potential sex maniac or in any way abnormal. It's nature's safety valve. Erections occur during certain phases of sleep and especially on waking in the morning.

Penis size may be a worry to both sexes but especially for the growing boy. Actually the size of the erect penis (usually about 5–7 inches or 12.7–17.7 cm long) matters little for providing sexual satisfaction for your female partner. Girth may be rather more important and this can increase by about 2 cm on erection so that it's better to be short and thick than long and thin. Nor does size of the erect penis bear a close relationship to its size when flaccid (nor to the size of your nose—another popular notion, although the nose is lined by similar tissues which can get engorged). This concern over penis size—or indeed whether it's crooked, too pointed, curved or something else—may only reflect an adolescent's sensitivity and feelings of inferiority and inadequacy. This is not to say that there aren't cases of 'micropenis' and other congenital and acquired abnormalities, but these are all very rare.

It's an interesting fact, of all the primates (our nearest cousins, monkeys, apes, etc.) man has by far the largest penis but nobody knows why this should be (for having intercourse in different positions?). In myth the gorilla is supposed to have a savage sex life; you will have noticed all those posters advertising King Kong films with the huge gorilla clutching a seductive girl. This may be used to symbolize man's 'animal' nature but in reality the gorilla has a tiny penis and a rotten sex life, mating about once a year and then with difficulty!

Because of the prominence of the male organ with its easy rousability and sensitivity to so many forms of stimulation, it's not surprising that boys soon learn to masturbate to orgasm. Even in our enlightened age there is still a great deal of ignorance about masturbation.

There are many popular names for it, the most emotive and condemnatory being the Victorian one of 'self-abuse'. Some others are playing with yourself, jerking off, tossing off and wanking.

A biblical reference (Genesis 38.8–11) which is still trotted out in this context, particularly as an example of divine wrath and punishment for masturbation, has been misunderstood. It is the story of Onan and the use of 'onanism' as a synonym for masturbation. But the 'real' sin of Onan was quite different. What he did was to break the Jewish Code, which made it obligatory for a man to marry his deceased brother's widow (i.e., sister-in-law). This Onan refused to do and his very mixed up feelings about this were shown when he attempted to have intercourse with her. He failed and 'spilled his seed on the ground' either because of coitus interruptus or more probably because of premature ejaculation, but not through masturbation.

This also highlights the continuing 'sacred' attitude towards seminal fluid, as being almost equivalent to life itself with the religious view that it is a sin to 'waste' it by any artificial means. This partly stems from ancient ideas about conception, when it was thought that the female played no vital part in this, except to 'house' the embryo.

You may think we are all so enlightened now that nobody really any longer feels guilty about masturbation. I recently saw a youth of 19 who had been involved in a car crash from which he received head injuries. He told me he thought the crash was his punishment from God because he had been masturbating. Masturbation is indulged in by practically all men at some time in their lives and by most women. It does not harm health, either mental, physical or sexual and leaves no tell tale marks, so that people cannot know you masturbate simply by looking at you. It can even be used to improve your sexual performance particularly in overcoming premature ejaculation. You can practise learning to postpone orgasm by masturbating until very near orgasm, stopping off just short, resting and starting again, repeating the process several times.

However, prolonged sexual stimulation without eventual orgasm can be very uncomfortable, even painful. Adolescent boys and young men who indulge in prolonged necking and petting or who are otherwise sexually aroused for long periods without relief, often experience this. It varies from a dull ache in the groins to painful, slightly tender testicles. Sometimes the pain has even been mistaken for appendicitis or a hernia. The 'cure' is to relieve the pelvic congestion by means of an orgasm.

Other adolescent changes may also cause embarrassment or worry. For instance, slight swelling of the breasts (quite normal—you're not changing sex!), the growth spurt and the voice breaking. To which could be added general shyness and clumsiness, blushing and acne. Agonies of indecision may result from group pressures to find yourself a girlfriend or to 'chat-up the birds'. Difficulties in this area can lead to further doubts about your masculinity—are you 'queer' or will others think so.

Fashions and ideas change, so that what a few years ago would have been considered cissy and effeminate may today be at the height of fashion—like long hair or wearing jewellery. But the main pressures on adolescents are to conform to their own standards, not to stand out from their friends, whatever their parents may think.

Feelings of inadequacy, sexually and otherwise, may lead you to try and impress by other means like doing 'daring' things such as taking a car away, smoking pot or some other minor delinquent act. There is a very strong element of male 'bonding' not shown by women. This is shown by such things as exclusively male clubs and other organizations and in the young by forming gangs, perhaps reinforced by that powerful symbol of virility, the motor bike, and wearing the right 'gear'.

Unfortunately this may well get associated with violence with an undercurrent of sexual frustration in the background. This is sometimes aided and abetted by one or two girl hangers-on rather like the 'groupies' who go with a male pop group. One of the worst manifestations of this gang mentality is the group rape or 'gang-bang', when one unfortunate girl is subjected to multiple rape.

Dating and keeping your own girlfriend becomes an important part of self-esteem although it may only be like having some other possession to show off to others. Love making, if that's the right term, may start as a quick grope in the back of a car and end disastrously with wet pants. Dancing can lead to an erection and similar results. But modern discos rarely encourage 'slow' dancing with an actual girl in your arms, it's more usually a ritual 'freak out' in a darkened noisy atmosphere. Conditions are made so that any normal form of communication is impossible—which is a good way of disguising the fact that the dancers are often so very lacking in social skills anyway.

But in one sense the male has to be 'aggressive' to complete the sex act; he has literally to stand-up for himself and penetrate his partner. So the real crux of male sexuality is to be able to do just this, with the accent on performance, achievement and possessing. This is often a difficult thing to achieve in our rather mixed up culture, as to some extent men are now encouraged to be more feminine and vice versa for females. In other words the traditionally more active dominant male and the passive female are no longer acceptable, or so we are told. But how much have 'ordinary' people really changed?

The more strident elements of the women's rights movements get a lot of publicity, so much so that the average woman who is quite content with her life, doesn't mind wearing a ring and being known as 'Mrs', is being made to feel unnecessarily guilty and upset by all this. The aspiring male feels even more unsure of himself; is he to be more loving, tender, caring and emotional and always say 'I love you' or be tough, assertive and go-getting? For a woman to 'call the tune', often in a provocatively challenging manner, demanding 'instant satisfaction' can be a very threatening situation indeed.

It used to be said that a man gives love to get sex and a woman gives sex to get love, but perhaps now we are trying to achieve a better balance. But if there is to be a radical alteration in sexual and gender roles then young children will have to be brought up accordingly. Young girls are still fed on 'romantic love' and look for long-term security; to be looked after, with the accent on responding and receiving. In boys it's sexual satisfaction, achievement, getting on top (literally and sexually— the superior position) with the search for the ideal housekeeper–mistress. The sex urge can be very strong in young men and as already noted is quickly and easily aroused, especially visually.

What is the young or indeed older single 'sex starved' male to do about his strong sexual urges, particularly if for some reason he can't find a suitable female partner? He may masturbate with or without the aid of sexy books or pictures. This can at least relieve tensions and be some outlet for unfulfilled fantasies. He can also go to a prostitute and so pay someone to give him sexual relief, but run the danger of getting V.D. He can, of course, seek help in trying to get himself a mate or adapt to celibacy.

Again, as a result of contemporary upheavals in traditional values, the whole question of marriage, settling down (or being 'tied-down') has been questioned. Why not just 'bum around' and take each day as it comes? This would include any casual sex that came your way. Or join some sort of 'squat' or commune, and share sex along with everything else. This rarely works as a permanent way of life but some young people do need to temporarily opt out to really find themselves.

One of the other traditional differences between the sexes and one that has led to a lot of misunderstanding is the belief that men are naturally more promiscuous. But it is not always made clear what is meant by this word. A parallel question to this is a slightly more sophisticated version of the same thing, namely, is man naturally monogamous?

To take the second proposition first. It is not possible to provide a satisfactory answer when put like this. It is more sensible to ask, is this particular pattern of marriage best suited to our society at this time? We tend to forget that others have different systems. If you study this throughout the world, in man and primates there are four basic patterns of mate (or sexual) selection:

1. Monogamy—one man and one woman with a life-long union and commitment.
2. Polygamy—the marriage of one man to two or more women.
3. Polyandry—the marriage of one woman to two or more husbands.
4. Promiscuity—a sexual free-for-all without exclusive rights to any one partner.

The first two are by far the most common. If you have the last arrangement, it doesn't matter if the female is attractive or not, nor does the male have to be dominant or fight off other potential mates. And, of course, sexual jealousy doesn't exist either. On the other hand there is the question of who looks after the children and whether you could run a twentieth century industrialized society on this basis.

It is interesting to note that in all animal polygamous societies the males are always larger than the females and more dominant. And in spite of recent views to the contrary one basic difference in humans is that, on average, males are always taller, larger and heavier than females. So in this sense polygamy would seem to be more 'natural' for us.

These systems need not be absolute, so you could have so-called 'serial monogamy' in which a couple are married and faithful to each other for a specified period of time and are then free to change (but what happens to the 'surplus' women?). Or, as seems to happen in many modern western societies, the system is outwardly a monogamous one but with an understanding that the more promiscuous male can have affairs on the side.

Promiscuity is really casual sex, sex without commitment, which is easier for the male both for reasons already mentioned and because he can much more readily dissociate sex from having a baby. But, as again already mentioned, it's much more difficult for a man to have 'sex on demand' and from the functional point of view women are better placed than men. Women can have multiple orgasms and in this sense could 'exhaust' a whole series of men in quick succession, something a man couldn't do with a series of women—so in this way women are 'naturally' more promiscuous.

Other people have tried to specify different types of promiscuity, like running two girlfriends at once or even thinking about another woman whilst having intercourse with your wife. A recent writer on the subject (Schofield)

63

has suggested several different types. The impersonal sort, who cares nothing for others but just uses them, in effect, for masturbation. Or promiscuity as a passing phase, like a holiday romance or as an exploratory stage in young people finding out about each other or even as a 'trial marriage'.

Yet another type is the man who is totally committed to his wife, would never dream of leaving her but needs change and variation in sexual experience. Occasionally promiscuity is compulsive; it is not enjoyed and not a pleasure, but a drive which he tries to overcome but finally has to give in to for temporary peace of mind. It can also be a symptom of mental illness, such as mania or, rarely, due to senile brain changes or mental handicap. Finally there is the sort that is deliberately engaged in as part of treatment, the so-called surrogate partner. For instance a single man with sexual problems is provided with a woman to help him overcome his difficulties but as part of a supervised treatment programme.

Throughout history there have been tales of famous womanisers such as the semi-legendary exploits of Don Juan and Cassanova and our modern 'heroes' of the cinema like James Bond. Mostly they are to be pitied rather than envied. They lead a restless, aimless sort of existence, using women as sexual objects, as conquests like a Red Indian with one more scalp to his belt. They are basically immature and insecure types, always trying to prove to themselves and to the world at large, how virile and manly they are. Paradoxically they may even be trying to overcome homosexual tendencies.

6

Coming Together

Even though I shall mostly refer to married couples, the actual sexual problems encountered could apply to any couple trying to get along together.

Sexual problems may begin soon after the 'public' commitment of getting engaged or sometimes things are fine until after the final commitment of marriage itself. Much depends on your background, sexual experience and reasons for getting married.

It is during engagement and courtship that doubts may begin to crop up, especially in the rather immature individual who is not quite sure whether he or she can really finally break with home and parents and set up on his own. This can be expressed in the form of an 'engagement neurosis', with minor neurotic symptoms e.g. of anxiety and indecisiveness in actually fixing the wedding date. Excuses are made for not doing so, like not having enough money or anywhere to live.

Sexual desire may be strong but perhaps there is still the fear of becoming pregnant and 'having' to get married, or sheer lack of opportunity for having intercourse, with consequent frustration and irritability. Some (girls particularly) still feel it's wrong to have intercourse before marriage. There may be unexpressed fears about the 'first time'.

Parental attitudes can still be very relevant. Do they approve of the chosen partner? Subtle or not so subtle pressures may be brought to bear, sometimes with financial inducements. A very possessive and dominating mother may see to it that her daughter lives close by and perhaps daughter, still a little unsure of herself, half agrees with this.

There can be such a build up to the honeymoon that both are so anxious that sexual performance certainly can suffer. The first intercourse can be disastrous or disappointing (and of course a blissful success!), especially if they feel they must consummate their marriage on the very first night whatever the circumstances. This may indeed be their first opportunity of complete freedom together but sometimes spoilt by the girl's sudden shyness, for instance about being undressed by her husband and appearing completely naked in front of him.

Intercourse may be attempted in the dark, for this sort of reason, and such a simple manoeuvre as the wife helping her husband insert his penis into her vagina not done because she wasn't sure about it. Or he may be worried in case he hurts her and so surprisingly and humiliatingly suddenly loses his erection or ejaculates all over the bed.

Most couples will have decided on what method of contraception to use long before the honeymoon and will also have some tentative plans about having children. The key to a happy and successful sex life is to be able to talk to each other about it; do not let it go by default as the one aspect of your lives that is never again mentioned. Sex itself is, after all, a form of communication, a way of expressing your love and desire for another person.

You can together find out what excites you, pleases you or disgusts you. Rather than read advanced manuals of sexual techniques as if your only aim in life was a gold medal in some sexual Olympics, try different forms of love play and arousal yourselves. Ideal notions of the 'good' lover do not always match up to real people. Old-fashioned ideas as to who should make the first move or of only using the 'missionary' position (man on top) may still hold sway.

Perhaps the greatest myth of all and hence one meaning of the title to this chapter is the idea that the ultimate goal is for you both to have orgasms simultaneously. It's very nice when it does happen but it can't always be so. This idea may place such a burden on the man that he can never really relax and enjoy himself and can make you both (unnecessarily) feel failures if this form of 'coming together' is not constantly achieved.

Some men get so desperate about this that they deliberately think about non-sexual or even nasty things when beginning intercourse to try and postpone ejaculation until their wife has had her orgasm.

You will soon discover from experience what turns each other on, how quickly each reaches orgasm and how to satisfy each other in the ways both like best. There are always individual differences but as a generalization it can be said that feeling and kissing a woman's breasts is far more exciting for the man. Also looking at her in the nude is more exciting than the other way round. Many men seem to think that their erect penis is exciting to a woman, whereas this is rarely so. In fact some girls may get rather a shock at their first sighting!

Personal hygiene is another factor. Obviously some are more fastidious than others. Some women only like men who are scruffy, not properly shaven and even dirty and sweaty—a sort of Lady Chatterley syndrome. As if the more neat, tidy, deodorized and smelling of after shave and talc he is, the more feminine i.e., like herself, which almost smacks of lesbianism. Some men find it exciting to have sex with their wives before rather than after a bath. It can be off putting if there is too much make-up and all the paraphernalia of taking it all off again at night and the 'do be careful of my hair' sort of response.

There is clearly a great deal of individual variation with some seeing sex as a rather smelly, messy business, the sort of thing you have before a nice hot bath. It is hard sometimes for a man to realize that even the most beautiful woman sweats, excretes and menstruates.

Some excessively prim women don't even like to touch themselves 'down there', so may not wash and dry themselves properly which in turn may favour an infection and discharge. Not wiping or washing your bottom properly, particularly if combined with nylon knickers and tights can lead to similar results. A bidet (not for washing the feet!) can be very helpful here.

These factors may also predispose towards 'honeymoon cystitis' in which the poor bride develops an infection of her urinary tract. This is shown by the frequent, painful passage of hot burning urine, some slight fever and general malaise. It can be a very painful and embarrassing condition, which prevents further intercourse as it becomes too sore and painful.

It may be triggered off by a very small injury, such as bruising, due to clumsy attempts at intercourse or be one form of an infection called non-specific urethritis. Occasionally a prolonged relapsing condition of chronic cystitis (inflammation of the bladder) is set up, although in some instances this gets confused with the frequent passage of small amounts of urine due to excessive nervousness and anxiety. If you do start getting symptoms like this, you should see your doctor about it.

Naturally one's ardour tends to die off after a time, but you may worry about how often you 'should' have intercourse. This varies enormously; it can start as high as 2–3 times a day but settling down some years later to the national average of once or twice a week, with

Friday and Saturday nights and Sunday mornings being peak times!

Some women complain that 'he never leaves me alone'. It is quite usual at the start of a marriage to go through a stage when you can't keep your hands off each other, perhaps more the husband off his wife. I've even had a patient complain that she couldn't get on with the washing up because her husband kept standing behind her and fondling her breasts!

Clearly the old cliché that marriage is a compromise has a lot of truth in it. You learn to adapt and meet each other's needs and desires. Other methods of sexual expression, apart from intercourse can be tried. Many a husband would like to experiment but is afraid to mention it in case his wife rejects him or thinks he's kinky. This is where greater understanding and good communication are so useful.

One obvious danger is that sexual relations deteriorate into a dull routine, a chore or even a duty. It is a difficult thing to achieve, living together for life and yet not getting tired, bored or irritated with each other. This is bound to happen at times. Sex—the giving or receiving of it—can also be used to express resentment and hostility, to humiliate and punish, because of failure to deal with other non-sexual problems in your marriage.

Being 'in love' may not be enough; do not forget other things such as companionship, interest in each other, a desire to please, help and encourage on a mutual basis and to face life's difficulties together. Nor is it enough just to share common interests and think the rest will all follow; simply liking Wagner and watercress is no guarantee of a happy union for evermore! On the other hand to share everything, never to have any secrets or a moment's privacy, can be too overwhelming as well as dull.

A man may secretly resent his wife being too independent and will object to her having her own job, himself wanting to be the bread winner. To some the old fashioned attitude of 'a woman's place is in the home' (usually meaning kitchen and bedroom!) is anathema. Or if he's been a mother's boy and never been allowed to lift a finger for himself, he may expect his wife to carry on doing the same. This may lead to sexual difficulties— either he idolizes her or sees her so much like mum, that sex is hard to reconcile with these attitudes.

The woman may have been spoilt by her father, overindulged and given everything she's asked for; she then transfers this dependency onto her husband. She may have learnt to be coy and flirtatious but never actually to 'give herself'. To marry too soon, in some cases seemingly to have missed out on adolescence altogether, is a kind of pseudo-maturity with the 'missed' rebellion and sowing of wild oats only coming on after some years of marriage. Also, of course, to marry the first person who comes along just to get away from an unhappy home is not usually a very good start either. Neither is marrying someone like a foreigner or a person very different from yourself just to 'show them' (parents, the establishment). It may then be difficult later on to admit your mistake, with the inevitable comeback 'I told you so'. Nor is marrying just because you're pregnant. The trouble is that people change and mature at different rates. The childhood sweetheart, the boy next door, your first and only girlfriend; you may be just right for each other at twenty, but very different by forty. But who can predict the future with such accuracy; if you wanted absolute certainty with no doubts or second thoughts whatsoever, very few marriages would ever take place.

How they are going to maintain sexual interest in each other hardly ever occurs to the newly married couple. Just to lie naked in each other's arms seems utter bliss. But the 'honeymoon period' cannot last forever. There are many other practical things to face such as money, jobs, illness, in-laws, accidents and ageing parents. There is also the problem of where to live. Starting married life in somebody else's house is not easy. Sexual intercourse may be marred by lack of privacy, thin walls, a squeaky bed or threat of interruptions.

If both partners are out working all day, then genuine tiredness and irritation can cause difficulties, particularly for the wife if she is expected to do two jobs, i.e., look after her husband as well. Barely expressed resentment may be shown by reluctance to have intercourse perhaps made worse in some wives by premenstrual tension.

The next problem is starting a family. This is more often by 'accident' than by careful planning. But if you think about it too carefully you'll find there is never a really convenient time to have a baby! If possible, though, you should allow yourselves time to get used to living together before introducing a third person.

A different sort of worry is when you have been 'trying' and no pregnancy results. This can cause a lot of unhappiness, bitterness and heart-searching. All sorts of wrong 'reasons' are thought of: previous masturbation, promiscuity or some other minor sexual peccadillo from the past. A wife may blame her husband and indeed she could be right as in about 40 per cent of cases of sub-fertility there is some disorder of the male sperm.

This situation can be a blow for both of you. A man's pride is hurt; after all a child is living proof of his virility and a woman's self-esteem takes a knock for not being a 'real' woman.

How long should you wait before seeking help? Much depends on your age but if you are young, round about 18 months to 2 years. As described under the rhythm method of contraception, you can take your own temperature to see if you are ovulating and also to make sure of having intercourse at around this time. It has been calculated that a highly fertile couple will conceive within about seven months of trying and roughly four out of five in a year. Of about 40,000 couples marrying every year, 5–6,000 face delay and disappointment; of these about a third can be helped by quite simple means and an increasing number by more sophisticated methods. However round about one couple in twenty must remain childless or be content with fewer children than they had hoped for. Sterility after one child may be involuntary or voluntary. In the former something may have gone wrong with the first birth or you may have been advised, on medical grounds, not to have any more.

Investigation of both partners is usually necessary, including a full sperm count. Temporary sterility may be due to keeping the testicles too hot, through wearing tight fitting nylon jockey-type briefs with tight trousers. Or a previous illness such as mumps or an accident may be responsible.

Surprisingly some couples are found who have never had proper intercourse; the wife may still have an intact hymen and without realizing it they may have been having intrafemoral (between the thighs or into the groin) intercourse for years.

Apart from putting right particular causes, other methods of treatment may have to be tried. 'Fertility drugs' may be indicated for secondary ovarian failure in order to induce ovulation. This is a very complicated subject and a number of special investigations are necessary. If successful there is about a 10 per cent risk of inducing a multiple pregnancy. Artificial insemination can be done either by using the husband's sperm (AIH) or from somebody else (AID—artificial insemination by donor). Specialist advice is needed over this. Adoption is, of course, another possibility. A number of women do eventually get pregnant after adoption, something difficult to explain.

A pregnancy may end in a miscarriage, usually before the third month. This can also cause a lot of distress particularly if it happens more than once. Should there be any restrictions on intercourse during pregnancy? Generally speaking no. However if there has been a miscarriage or if the woman does have a little 'show' of blood, it is wise to avoid intercourse until after the third month and at the times of missed periods.

Later in pregnancy intercourse can become physically difficult, at least in the traditional position. Other positions should be tried, like rear entry with the woman on her side. Provided she is well (early pregnancy may be marred by sickness and late pregnancy by backache, the middle three months usually being the best time) and the pregnancy normal, intercourse is all right. But once labour has started or when the waters have broken it should be avoided.

Many pregnant women worry about losing their looks and attractiveness for their husband, so regular intercourse is a further boost to morale. Men vary in their reactions, some being positively turned on while others who, although still loving and caring, can barely conceal their dislike of the bulging figure. It is a traditional time for husbands to be unfaithful.

Some husbands get so involved in the pregnancy— part envy, part sympathy—that they too develop pregnancy 'symptoms', especially abdominal pain, and diarrhoea, particularly at the time of labour (couvade syndrome). Whether husbands should be present at the birth is a matter of personal preference and discussion with your doctor or midwife.

73

After childbirth many women go through a very emotional patch, when they easily get a bit weepy and down (maternity 'blues'); there is an old saying that 'as soon as the milk begins to flow so do the tears'. She can also be a bit sore, especially if she's had an episiotomy. This is a small cut made in the perineum to enlarge the vaginal opening for the passage of the baby's head. After the birth this is stitched up and may cause a little pain on first resuming intercourse.

Also, of course, coping with a newborn baby is a very tiring and disruptive business. A rather immature husband may feel his nose put out of joint a bit, as his wife seems to have switched all her love and attention from him onto the baby. What with this, very little sex and possibly sleepless nights as well, it can be a difficult time all round.

Usual contraceptive precautions should be taken after childbirth as pregnancy can still result even when breast feeding. There is a lot of controversy about breast feeding itself, the final decision must rest with the mother on the advice of her doctor. Some women are very embarrassed by it and this is not helped in our culture by the breasts being of such sexual significance. It is an interesting fact that in primates (apes and monkeys) the female does not develop her breasts until after pregnancy. In the human, for reasons which are not really clear, breast development is completed at a relatively early age and becomes a vital part of those vital statistics!

Breast size is no guide to milk yield. Breast feeding will not ruin the figure; changes in the breasts occur during pregnancy anyway with darkening of the area around the base of the nipples and usually some 'stretch marks' as well. A few women find the whole business rather messy and 'animal' whilst others get the most intense pleasure from feeding, including sexual pleasure. This is quite normal and no cause for alarm or guilt.

Another reason why women may not be so keen on sex after childbirth, particularly if they've had a rather bad time, is the fear of 'falling' again. This is even more reason for good contraceptive advice.

7

Coming Apart

In this chapter, I want to discuss the causes of unsuccessful intercourse. It will make it easier to understand
if, to begin with, I take male and female problems
separately, realizing that they obviously affect each other
(for instance, if a man 'comes' too early his partner
could be left frustrated without having had a chance to
reach orgasm).

First a look at some of the terms used. I am very much
against the use of the word 'frigid' to describe a woman
who has difficulty in achieving orgasm. It is really a rather
insulting word, often used by men who get angry with
women who tease them or who are unresponsive to their
advances. Women's Lib supporters add to the emotional
atmosphere by stating there aren't any frigid women
anyway, only incompetent male lovers.

A woman who seemingly cannot have an orgasm may
well be a very warm, friendly, sexually attractive person
and in no way cold, aggressive or rejecting. The rather
more cumbersome but neutral description of 'orgasmic
dysfunction' will be used in preference to 'frigid'. Also
to call somebody 'inadequate', even when not intended in
this way, seems to imply a value judgement, so is also best
avoided.

Vaginismus is used to describe a spasm of the muscles
surrounding the vagina, which in extreme cases involves
the thighs and legs as well, so that sexual intercourse becomes physically impossible. These spasms are involuntary and there is no truth in the myths that a woman can
'rape' a man this way, that his penis can be injured or

they become locked together during intercourse and can be separated only by giving her a general anaesthetic. These things happen only in fiction and not in real life.

Vaginismus is one cause of a marriage not being consummated. Non-consummation is the commonist cause for a marriage to be dissolved on the grounds of nullity. Other grounds for this are a partner of the same sex (diagnosed by chromosomes), undisclosed epilepsy, V.D., mental illness, pregnancy at the time of marriage by another man or one spouse below the age of consent.

Impotence is a general term referring to a man's inability to successfully perform sexual intercourse. Some doctors like to restrict its use to difficulties in getting and maintaining an erection. Dyspareunia is the medical name for painful intercourse.

We are now in a position to describe and classify in more detail the various types of sexual dysfunction that commonly occur.

In the male these are:

1. Loss of libido or lack of sexual desire
2. Difficulties in obtaining and maintaining an adequate erection
3. Premature ejaculation
4. Slow or absent ejaculation
5. Dyspareunia

All these disorders may be further subdivided into primary—that is, have never been right— and secondary, at one time all right but subsequently failed. Finally by the way in which they start, into acute or sudden onset, and insidious, or very slow, over a period of time.

Now it's important to realize that practically all men have been impotent on some occasion in their lives. This is to be expected when we take into account the delicate balance of the nervous and other factors involved. There are many possible causes of impotence, some obvious and some not quite so obvious and it may well require a thorough examination and investigation by your doctor or a specialist to sort it out. Sometimes, even after the most exhaustive tests, no cause can be found. Many cases are transient and right themselves; it's the persistent ones that cause so many problems.

The main causes of male impotence can be divided into a) physical b) drugs c) psychological d) situational or e) any combination of these.

Physical causes are relatively rare but impotence can be associated with sugar diabetes, liver disease, some nervous (neurological) diseases and following some surgical operations such as prostatectomy or on the lower bowel. Too little testosterone (male sex hormone) is an uncommon cause. When impotence is part of a physical illness the loss of sexual desire or function is usually overshadowed by other symptoms. Being very overweight, or generally unfit can be contributing factors.

Dyspareunia or painful intercourse may be due to some local disorder of the penis such as a too tight foreskin, disease of the blood vessels or a hernia. Intercourse may be impossible due to back pain or hip trouble.

There are a large number of drugs available which can adversely affect either desire or performance. The commonest is alcohol, which is not, as frequently supposed, a brain stimulant but a depressant. In small doses it may cause loss of inhibitions and anxiety and so seem to stimulate desire. In larger doses it can produce loss of erection, premature ejaculation or delayed ejaculation. The drunken porter in Shakespeare's *Macbeth* put it well when he said, about the effects of alcohol: 'Lechery, sir, it provokes and unprovokes; it provokes the desire, but it takes away the performance'.

Barbiturates ('barbs') and other types of sleeping pills, if abused, can have similar effects. Hallucinogens such as LSD ('acid') are very unpredictable and a 'bad trip' can be a terrifying experience. Marijuana ('pot', 'hash', 'joints') is claimed by some to enhance sexual fantasies and sensations but there are no controlled studies on this. Stimulants such as the amphetamines ('speed') may initially cause some increased excitement and apparently better performance but are highly addictive with bad consequences to your physical (including sexual) and mental health. This applies even more so to the 'hardstuff' (heroin, cocaine).

However there are drugs prescribed by doctors for other complaints which can cause impotence. For example, some drugs given to control high blood pressure or some of the tranquillisers and antidepressants used in psychiatry. There are also drugs which are specifically designed to stop men feeling randy such as the oestrogens or the newer anti-androgen preparations. Very occasionally certain compounds containing toxic chemicals, used in industry or farming, may be responsible.

The commonest cause of all is psychological, due to anxiety upsetting the nervous balance of erection and ejaculation. Anxiety is often at its height when you first have intercourse, when engaged or on your honeymoon. Although once failure has been experienced it is only too easy for a vicious circle to develop in which worrying about it happening again next time very often causes it to do just that. This 'anticipatory anxiety' with further anxiety and fear of failure piles on the agony and helps to perpetuate the condition. Taking alcohol to try and overcome this doesn't help either.

Mental depression, from whatever cause, is very commonly accompanied by loss of libido. This is usually fairly obvious and is only part of a general loss of

79

interest. Other psychological or emotional 'hang-ups' may well be present and need more expert sorting out, especially if satisfactory sexual intercourse has never been achieved.

By 'situational' I mean relative impotence so that, for instance, a man is impotent with his mistress but not with his wife or vice versa, proving he can 'do it' when circumstances are right. The first situation is more common than might be expected—with the added excitement, perhaps tinged with guilt and the actual physical circumstances, premature ejaculation can easily result. Occasionally a man is impotent with his wife and as an experiment tries with another woman to see if it makes any difference.

Just how his wife reacts to his impotence is of crucial importance. This may vary from sympathetic understanding and help to outright rejection, hostility and accusations that he must have stopped loving her or be getting his sex 'elsewhere'. It is the greatest possible blow to male pride—a most embarrassing, humiliating and depressing experience, especially if desire is still there but cannot be expressed.

If he is further humiliated by his wife, for example by her making snide comments, ringing him at work to enquire 'are you a man or a mouse?', or hinting to friends and neighbours and making jokes about it in public, he will only get worse. She may also misinterpret the fact that he still gets erections in the morning or during sleep as evidence that he must be having erotic dreams about other women yet he can't make love to her. These erections are more or less automatic and have nothing to do with his real feelings towards his wife.

But as impotence itself can be an expression of underlying tensions and hostility, reflecting all sorts of unsatisfactory personal relationships, it is sometimes difficult to work out cause and effect. Clearly, though, if you are having other sexual outlets, for example masturbating a lot, there will be less desire left for your wife. Occasionally there are homosexual problems which you may have hoped would go away but have persisted without your fully realizing it.

Both novelty and familiarity can present problems. If you have been away for a long time it may take a little while to get used to each other again. After many years of marriage, familiarity, monotony, and boredom with the same partner, perhaps coupled with waning sexual desire, may be responsible for both lack of desire and poor performance. Men sometimes think it's entirely up to their wives to be always appealing and sexually attractive without realizing their own deficiencies in this respect.

Lack of consideration and understanding of each other's fears and needs can be aggravating factors. A wife commonly complains that her husband is 'unromantic', will never say 'I love you' or be demonstrative except perhaps with presents. He is too eager for intercourse without first 'wooing' her. One woman complained to me that her husband 'bobbed on and off me like a rabbit'.

Men tend to be at a bit of a disadvantage here as so frequently they are brought up not to be 'sloppy', sentimental or 'cissy'. Also because of traditional teaching the woman may not like to initiate love making in case it's regarded as being too 'forward' or it's not what nicely brought up ladies do. As a man gets older he needs more stimulation and as a woman gets older she needs more attention, praise and encouragement.

Of all the forms of male impotence mentioned the most common is premature ejaculation, which can be virtually lifelong and persistent or happen only very occasionally with one particular person or only in certain situations. Ejaculation occurs either before penetration, during attempts at it or immediately afterwards. Because of the 'refractory period' it is not possible to get another erection or perform again straight away.

In acute onset erectile impotence there is an inability to obtain or maintain an erection for long enough to conclude intercouse to orgasm and ejaculation. You can start out with a good erection but then it suddenly goes. In older age groups, greater stimulation is necessary for arousal and erection is not usually at such an acute angle as in younger men.

In the insidious onset type a not uncommon story is that of a man in his 40s, who has never been very highly sexed, perhaps married rather late in life and who has gradually over the past few years got such poor erections that he's almost given up trying to have intercourse any more. In some of these cases no convincing causes can be found and the outlook is poor.

Normally speaking ejaculation and orgasm go together. Sometimes the problem is a persistent inability to experience orgasm or to ejaculate in the presence of normal erection and desire. Unlike other forms of impotence this is rarely complained of by the female partner as it is akin to coitus reservatus and so gives her ample opportunity to reach her climax. However it can be very frustrating for a man. Actual 'dry-run' orgasm without ejaculation is possible but rare. Very occasionally due to an anatomical fault or after prostatectomy the seminal fluid is passed out backwards into the bladder and not ejaculated externally in the usual way.

So you will now realize that there are different forms of impotence with many possible causes and for all but the most simple and obvious ones medical advice will be needed. This will inevitably involve your partner as well. The sooner you both go for advice the better.

In women orgasmic dysfunction may also take several forms and, as in the male, can be either primary (never been right) or secondary. Similarly it may have come on acutely and suddenly, or more gradually over a period of time, and the trouble can also be random or situational.

The degree of dysfunction or impairment of your pleasure can vary enormously, from total repugnance to all your partner's advances ('I can't even bear him to touch me') to enjoyment of intercourse without an actual climax. Occasionally orgasm never has been and never will be experienced, in spite of normal desire and adequate stimulation. In others there may be a degree of physical immaturity, with a late puberty and poorly developed secondary sexual characters, with no orgasm until relatively late in life, say age 35–40. Sometimes too, there is poor lubrication of the vagina which makes intercourse difficult or even painful.

Upbringing, personality, the state of the marriage are, as with male problems, important background factors. A temporary state of loss of libido may follow childbirth or such operations as hysterectomy. Loss of libido may also occur in depression, general ill-health with or without anaemia, fatigue or some infection of the genital tract. Not so much is known about the effects of drugs on female libido but in some cases a contraceptive pill may cause some loss of interest and response.

Clearly, adequate stimulation by a loving partner, proper contraceptive precautions and the right situation are all desirable. General tension, resulting from all sorts of worries, or an anxiety neurosis are other possible factors.

Dyspareunia or painful intercourse may result from 'deep' pain after penetration or be more superficially caused by dryness or vaginismus. A local infection or other minor gynaecological troubles can be responsible.

An extreme degree of immaturity often coupled with hysterical features in a woman's personality are the basic ingredients for the 'tease' or more crudely the 'prick-tease'. This is a superficially seductive woman who likes to arouse and tease men but then refuses to deliver the goods. It is this type more than any other that gets labelled 'frigid'. She makes a good short-term flirt but a poor long term partner, as she is incapable of a mature and lasting relationship.

She may have been spoilt as a child, overindulged by her father and never able to identify with her mother. She ends up by really despising men and seeks to humiliate them as well as being extremely insecure in her own (biological) female role. Denial of sexual satisfaction, both to herself and to men, is then used to punish and express this hostility. Some of this 'philosophy' is self-fulfilling because by and large she will only attract a weak and neurotic man who is unsure about his own masculinity, and by her seductive behaviour will cause a lot of men to make a pass at her. She can then say men are all the same, all they want is one thing.

Closely allied is the so-called 'castrating woman', that is a woman who envies men but spends her whole life disparaging them and undermining their self-confidence. She can also be responsible for inducing impotence in her male partners. A classical example of the seductive-destructive woman is Delilah who, you will remember from the Bible (Judges 16), seduced and betrayed Samson and symbolically castrated him by cutting off his hair.

If such women do marry, sexual problems inevitably follow, although these may be partly overcome by 'mate selection'. For example she may marry a weak and passive husband, who is then 'rewarded' for staying that way by such remarks as 'my husband is so good, he never bothers me'. When hearing this one should ask oneself why not? However, husband and wife may change in different directions as they grow older, so that 'the worm can turn'. Life indeed can begin at forty, but it's when the previously quiet and submissive man begins to assert himself both sexually and otherwise, that the trouble starts. His wife may then react by getting 'depressed'.

The male equivalent, sometimes called psychopathic or an abnormally aggressive personality is sexually opportunist, simply using women for his own sexual pleasure, again rather despising them for being weak and 'giving in'. He has no thoughts for her satisfaction. Fidelity would be impossible and far from being devious and secretive he may well openly boast about his conquests and humiliate his wife by telling her how his other women are so much better in bed. At the same time he may well insist on his 'rights', and make his wife indulge in all sorts of sexual activities which disgust her.

Jealousy can adversely affect sexual adjustment in a marriage at any stage. It is a difficult emotion to define but clearly there is a 'normal' element of possessiveness and potential jealousy in all exclusively monogamous marriages. Jealousy may become a problem either because it's irrational and unfounded or over-intense and exaggerated.

Freud suggested that several different emotions were involved. Grief over the loss of your loved one, pain due to wounded pride, feelings of hatred towards the successful rival and self-criticism in holding yourself accountable for the loss.

Jealousy arises out of insecurity, mistrust and feelings of inferiority. It occurs more often in certain types of people and is much more common in men. The sort of person who tends to be either excessively fussy and perfectionistic, where everything is black or white, who maintains there must be a cause for everything and there is no such thing as chance or coincidence is often jealous.

So, too, is the basically mistrustful and suspicious sort, who could never accept others at face value, tends to get hold of the wrong end of the stick and always seems to have a 'chip on his shoulder'.

The actual jealousy is based on 'projection', a technical term borrowed from psychoanalysis, which means an inability to recognize your own faults, which instead you 'project' onto others, so that really you don't trust yourself. Sexual jealousy can take many forms: for instance, the woman who naively expects that after marriage her husband will never look at another woman and when he does, gets all upset. This may even extend from looking at real women to looking at pictures in books or magazines or immediately switching off television if a pretty woman comes on (he's never allowed to watch 'Miss World'!). Another way is to falsely accuse him of having it off with another woman because he is temporarily impotent.

Once the idea gets implanted in your mind even the most innocent and trivial things begin to assume sinister proportions. One patient I had was afraid to put on a clean shirt or use aftershave lotion as this meant to his jealous wife he was going to see his mistress that day. Another case, the other way round, was that of a husband who looked through his wife's bag before she went to work, to discover lipstick and deodorant, which to him implied she was going to meet her lover at lunchtime.

In more extreme cases still, all of which I've met, a husband hired a private detective to follow his wife; another insisted on sending her knickers to the public analyst to see if seminal stains could be detected; and another still made his wife strip completely naked for inspection every time she'd been out without him. Further doubts about possible paternity of his children may torment the jealous husband. Sometimes a wife makes a mistake of 'confessing' to a non-existent affair in the hope that it will shut him up, but it doesn't. Another form of jealousy is not concerned with the here and now or the immediate future, but the past. An intense pre-occupation and ridiculous jealousy over his wife's previous boyfriends, even back to times before he'd even met her.

Violent arguments can ensue and even murder be committed either of the supposedly unfaithful wife or her 'lover'. In the really pathological cases there is nearly always evidence of other personality problems and the situation may be made worse by alcoholism. In the instances where there actually has been some infidelity, he may never forgive her and go on about it so much that the marriage eventually breaks up.

But extra-marital affairs are common. A recent (1970) American estimate was that about half of all married men and a quarter of all married women will have intercourse outside marriage at one time or another. What happens to the marriage as a consequence very much depends on the personalities and backgrounds of the spouses. Certainly one reason why a couple come for help over a sexual problem, whether it be vaginismus or impotence, is the fear that the spouse will 'go elsewhere' if something isn't done. On the other hand some seemingly very mature couples can give each other 'carte blanche' about affairs and yet continue in a loving relationship with each other.

Others still may make certain stipulations or conditions, such as, 'as long as I don't know about it' or 'as long as you're not in love with her'. Some wives expect their husbands to be unfaithful to them, for instance on long business trips abroad, but this is never actually put into words. It can even help an ailing marriage which perhaps has got stuck into a rather routine and monotonous sex life yet both still love each other. It gives the man a 'new lease of life' which in turn helps him to behave better towards his wife (there may of course be an element of guilt in this).

Some women resent not the actual sex he's having but the deception, the disloyalty, the time involved (which could have been spent with her or the children) or even the money he's spending on 'her'. But in real life, in spite of the whole tradition of romantic love being based on adulterous love, these 'brief encounters' can be full of snags. This is especially so if you are both married and all four live in the same small town. The 'romance' is so often spoilt both by practical difficulties like finding a suitable rendezvous and alibi, as well as by lies, guilt, remorse, furtiveness and frustration.

As already mentioned this can sometimes be in the nature of an experiment. For instance, in the case of the non-orgasmic wife, to find out if it's her 'fault' or something to do with her husband. But when she does find that she has a splendid orgasm with the television repair man, what then?

In a recent survey of people attending marriage guidance counsellors the ten most common complaints of the husbands and wives, in order of priority were: lack of communication, constant arguments, unfulfilled emotional needs, sexual dissatisfaction, financial disagreements, in-law trouble, infidelity, conflicts about children, domineering spouse and suspicious spouse.

Being 'oversexed' is not such a common cause for complaint. It is sometimes just a matter of degree, a misunderstanding, or reflection of the couple's relationship. One woman complained to me that her husband was a 'sex maniac' (her words). When I asked in what way, she said 'he wants sex with the light on'!

Some semi-technical terms which are bandied about in this connection are nymphomania (Greek 'nympha', a bride; also the name for the inner lips of the vulva) for excessive desire in women and satyriasis in the male (from satyr—a mythical beast, half human, half goat, noted for its lasciviousness). Occasionally the term eroto-mania is used in psychiatry for a pathological pre-occupation with erotic fantasies or activities. In its most extreme form a woman may hold the delusional belief that she is loved by a famous person.

Compulsive or anxiety driven sexual overactivity may form part of a psychiatric illness, as may very unin-hibited sexual activity and demands. Such behaviour, particularly when completely out of character, may be due to an abnormally elevated mood as part of a manic-depressive illness. But apparent 'oversexiness' can hide chronic frustration and dissatisfaction, a continuing attempt to find relief in an orgasm which is never properly accomplished.

On the other hand I have had patients who keep on experiencing orgasms without much in the way of external stimulation, with no lasting relief from masturbation or other sexual activity. Occasionally this is part of a physical illness such as a rare type of epilepsy. This is certainly the case with priapism—which is prolonged, painful and unwanted erections, with no accompanying sexual desire. A painful bending of the erect penis to one side (chordee) may be due to previous gonorrhoea or in the 40–60 age group as a result of a rare condition called Peyronie's disease.

It is not uncommon for there to be an upsurge of libido and sexual activity at the time of the menopause. Apart from the hormonal changes this could be as a result of no longer fearing pregnancy or as a sort of 'last fling' just to prove to yourself that you're not growing old and are still attractive.

Many a woman quite unnecessarily fears 'the change', and imagines that all sorts of terrible things will happen to her like becoming fat and ugly, growing a moustache, losing all sexual desire and attractiveness. But only a minority get any severe symptoms, with most 'working class' women just getting on with it, accepting it as a part of life just as they did the start of their periods.

In recent years there has been a lot of publicity given to replacement hormone (oestrogen) therapy, not only to relieve the 'symptoms' of the menopause but in some quarters it has been greeted almost as an elixir of life for perpetual youth. Hormonal attempts at 'rejuvenation' have a long history, in both sexes. Before a lot was known about hormones, 'monkey gland' (a euphemism for testis) transplants were advocated for the male, but don't work; nor does 'topping up' with testosterone (the male hormone).

There is the ancient idea of the rejuvenation of an old man by a young woman. The biblical King David tried it by inhaling the breath of young girls. It seems to work with rats, though; if you put a young female in with a group of old males, then with or without actual sexual contact, the males will live longer.

If there are demonstrable hormone deficiencies at the menopause, then replacement therapy could well help. It's rather like taking a contraceptive pill long after you need it to prevent conception. What the oestrogen will do is to stop the vagina going too dry (which will help intercourse), stop hot-flushes and sweats and possibly slow up the thinning of your bones. This is about all. You should have a thorough medical check-up and discuss the various advantages and disadvantages with your doctor.

The male menopause or 'mid-life crisis' is not associated with any dramatic changes in hormone levels and is more psychological. You become concerned with taking stock of achievements and missed opportunities, ambitions, self-esteem and career, with the realization that there are big changes ahead like retirement.

Actually levels of testosterone depend on the amount of sexual activity, so the best way of keeping your sex life going is to keep going! You may also be tempted to have a last fling or you suddenly make a fool of yourself by falling in love with your secretary (who unfortunately treats you like a father figure!).

We have already noted certain normal changes that take place with increasing age. Ejaculation as well as other components of the total sexual act do alter with age. These alterations cause more worry to some than to others, for instance, those who are anxious, sensitive, introspective and very set in their ways.

Factors which may impair the pleasure of sexual intercourse in the older man are:

1. Fatigue, particularly mental.
2. Boredom and monotony associated with the same partner over many years.
3. Preoccupation with career, retirement or economic position.
4. Over-eating and excessive drinking.
5. Physical or mental changes either in himself or his partner, e.g., obesity, depression.
6. Fear of failure and preoccupation with his own inadequacy.

Another aggravating factor in men is enlargement of the prostate gland, which initially causes trouble with passing water. Other disabilities, such as arthritis, may also make things more difficult. It is only recently that the sexual needs of the handicapped (mentally or physically or both) have become recognized, openly discussed and attempts made to do something about it.

It is certainly a true test of a marriage if you can still get on well together following retirement and when the children have grown up and left home. You are thrown together again, with time on your hands. An ideal opportunity for a second honeymoon? Some women suffer from the 'empty nest syndrome', but this may be partly obviated by having grandchildren. But, as already pointed out there is no reason why you should not have an active sex life for the rest of your days, if that is what you both want. But once stopped, particularly in the male, it's very difficult to start again. It is a very undangerous form of activity and exercise, so don't be put off by over-cautious doctors. If you've had a heart attack or a serious operation, as soon as you are allowed to be up and about again and you feel like it then you can resume some sexual activity. You will have to see for yourself what sort of sexual activity you can manage, being guided by such things as slight chest pain, breathlessness or a very rapid heart beat.

On the other hand if you both agree that the time has come to stop, don't force yourselves to continue having intercourse just because you feel you ought to. Close physical contact may well be enough.

8

A Pox on You?

There is a whole group of diseases, spread by sexual contact, called the Sexually Transmitted Diseases. Three of these—syphilis, gonorrhoea and chancroid—are 'officially' described as Venereal Diseases (V.D.) by an Act of Parliament. They have an interesting history.

The word venereal comes from 'venery' which means the pursuit of Venus, the goddess of love. These diseases are probably as old as man although their origins are still disputed. The word gonorrhoea literally means 'a flow of seed'. It probably existed long before it was first fully described in the second century A.D.

Indeed it's possible that Moses had a lot of trouble with it, as many of the Children of Israel, on their way to the Promised Land, were infected. His soldiers possibly contracted the disease from women taken prisoner after a battle.

The organism causing syphilis is closely related to one which can be found in the soil. This may have been its origin millions of years ago. It may then have got into animals and finally man. The first we really know about it in Europe was a big epidemic in the sixteenth century. It was thought to have been brought back from America by the sailors who went with Christopher Columbus. Others think it might have originated in Africa.

The name comes from a poem called 'Syphilis sive Morbus Gallicus' (Syphilis or the French disease) written in 1530 by an Italian poet-physician called Girolamo Fracastoro. In this poem there is a shepherd called Syphilus, who is struck down by a dreadful disease as a punishment for offending the gods. It soon acquired many other names, the most popular being the Great Pox (as opposed to smallpox) or as the first cases were described in French soldiers, the French disease. But because of an increasing stigma attached to it, no one wished to be identified with it so that it has also been called the Christian Disease (by the Turks) as well as the Neapolitan, Portuguese, German, Spanish, Syrian, Egyptian and English Disease!

By the seventeenth and eighteenth centuries both gonorrhoea and syphilis were rife and often confused by doctors. An eighteenth-century surgeon, John Hunter, made experiments on himself. He innoculated his own penis with pus from a man known to have gonorrhoea only to find he had contracted syphilis as well, from which he subsequently died. This tragic lesson is still very relevant today as you can have both infections at once, although one may mask the other.

Gonorrhoea or 'the clap' is now an extremely common infection, about as common in fact as measles. The bacteria that causes it can only survive outside the human body for a very few minutes, so gonorrhoea cannot be caught from a lavatory seat! It is transmitted during sexual intercourse or close genital contact. The bacteria can also survive in the mouth and pharynx and cause 'sexual sore throat' or oral gonorrhoea.

Symptoms usually start a few days after infection but may take several weeks. One very important point to note and this cannot be stressed too often is that anything up to 70 per cent of infected women may have no obvious symptoms. They remain carriers and are able to infect others for up to a year or more. There is no lasting immunity from gonorrhoea, so you can catch it again and again.

The initial symptoms in men are a thick yellowish-green

discharge from the urethra, accompanied by the frequent, painful passage of urine. Sometimes the urine is blood-stained. The discharge is most apparent first thing in the morning. If untreated the infection can spread to involve the epididymis and bladder. Occasionally a stricture of the urethra, abscesses and infection of the prostate gland can occur. The net result may be subfertility or sterility. In rare cases the joints and heart are affected and a form of meningitis has also been described.

In homosexuals the anus is a frequent site of infection when there is an anal discharge, a burning pain with blood and pus passed in the motions.

In women it is much more difficult to detect, yet vital to do so as the complications (apart from infecting others) can be so serious. There can be urinary symptoms, as in the male, soreness and inflammation around the vaginal opening and a vaginal discharge. The infection can spread back to infect the anus without there having been anal intercourse. The mouth and pharynx can also be infected.

Pain in the lower abdomen may indicate salpingitis (infection of the tubes which if left untreated can go on to peritonitis and cause sterility). One estimate for resulting sterility was about 500 women a year. Gonorrhoea may also be passed on to her children by an infected mother. This can affect the newborn baby's eyes, causing one sort of 'sticky eyes'. A very unhygienic mother may also occasionally infect her very young daughter (age 2–5) causing an inflammation of the child's vulva and vagina.

The highest rate of infection for gonorrhoea occurs in the age group 20–24 when there are about 12 men to every 7 women infected. Up to age 19 there are more girls than boys infected. The actual figures for England in 1974 were for the age group up to age 19, females 7,003, males 4,772. Aged under 16, girls 460 cases and boys 118. If detected early it can be completely cured, either by penicillin or some other antibiotic.

Fortunately syphilis ('the pox', 'bad blood') is now relatively rare. For the whole of England in 1974 there were 1,648 new cases of primary and secondary syphilis, with five times as many men as women infected. It is the most dangerous form of V.D. and can be fatal in its later stages. A large proportion of cases are now found amongst homosexuals in our larger cities. If not diagnosed and treated early it progresses through four increasingly serious stages.

After the primary and secondary stages it passes into a dormant phase when there may be no symptoms at all. It can then flare up again, anything from 5–50 years later to produce a chronic, crippling and killing disease. In Britain something like 200 people a year die from syphilis. In the first three stages a pregnant woman can pass on the disease to her unborn child, to produce congenital syphilis.

In the first or primary stage, one or more sores or ulcers, which are completely painless (and hence tend to be ignored) appear on or in the sex organs, or other places, depending on the site of the infection. This can be penis, vulva, vagina, anus, mouth or even a finger. It usually takes three weeks to appear. Lumps may be formed near the site of the infection, e.g., in the groins, due to lymph glands getting infected. These are part of the body's defences against any infection.

Whether treated or not, the ulcers eventually heal; but if untreated the germs spread into the bloodstream and can eventually land up in any tissue or part of the body. This is the secondary stage. This usually shows itself by the appearance of a non-itchy rash somewhere on the body, sores in and around the mouth, throat or sex organs with general signs of a fever, such as headache, rise in temperature and general aches and pains. Again if untreated this stage can wax and wane for a long time but eventually disappears.

We are now in the third or latent stage of hidden syphilis, which can only be detected by special blood tests. Because the germs can get to any part of the body, via the bloodstream, many different symptoms are possible. This is why medical students are taught that syphilis is the great mimic and to think about it as a possible cause for all sorts of illnesses, from heart to bone disease, paralysis to blindness.

In the fourth and last stage, the brain and nervous system are involved and generally speaking so much damage caused as to be irreversible, although further progress can usually be halted. The resulting condition is called GPI for short, or general paralysis of the insane. Many years ago this was quite a common condition in mental hospitals but is now quite rare.

Routine blood tests are done on all pregnant women attending antenatal clinics and also on all blood collected from blood donors before being used for transfusion. If found in the first three stages syphilis can be completely cured.

The commonest cause of a vaginal discharge is a tiny one-celled organism called trichomonas. In men it may cause an urethral discharge but this is rare; men are usually 'carriers', harbouring the organism but without any symptoms. It can be passed on by sexual intercourse and just possibly, because it can live for a while in damp conditions, from lavatory seats. It is also possible that some mothers may infect their baby girls at birth, the organisms then lying dormant until the 'teens or later.

It can produce a nasty inflammation of the vagina, with a yellowish smelly discharge. This causes general itchiness and irritation around the vulva and discomfort on passing water. It can cause great misery and embarrassment, unnecessarily so because it can be readily diagnosed by special tests and completely cured by a course of tablets. These are usually prescribed for the regular partner as well, to prevent reinfection.

Probably the commonest cause now of urethritis in men is so-called non-specific urethritis or NSU; this is sometimes called NGU or non-gonococcal urethritis. Symptoms are practically confined to men, producing the frequent and painful passage of urine and a discharge. The name 'non-specific' comes from the fact that, although it has all the characteristics of an infection, in many cases no particular germ can be isolated. Occasionally one from inside the bladder is responsible or a trichomonas. Other theories have suggested a virus or a type of allergy. It is not caused by having intercourse during a menstrual period.

Somewhere between 1–3 per cent of men with NSU develop complications, which can involve the eyes and joints (arthritis). Early treatment is essential and even when a specific germ cannot be found, some of the newer more powerful antibiotics may effect a cure.

Other conditions will only be mentioned briefly. Vaginal thrush is medically known as candidiasis, after the name of the fungus responsible for the infection. It is often found in the mouth, on the skin and in the vagina of healthy people and is not necessarily spread by sexual intercourse. It may suddenly flare up and cause symptoms without obvious cause or in association with pregnancy, diabetes, taking the contraceptive pill or other drugs. It then produces a thick creamy white discharge and itchiness. Anal infection can also occur. It is much more rare in men but is one possible cause of balanitis, infection and soreness around the glans penis and under the foreskin. It can usually be cured.

Genital herpes or 'cold sores' of the sexual organs is a

virus infection similar in type to the more common sort on the lips. The first attack in women can be quite severe, with general signs of fever and pain and occasionally ulceration of the vulva and vagina. This usually settles in a few weeks but recurrences are likely. It can also affect the penis, with swelling of the glands in the groin. If got early enough in the first attack cure is possible.

Genital warts are also caused by a virus and can be infectious. The virus tends to grow rapidly in the warm moist areas in and around the genital and anal regions of both sexes. It is not a form of cancer. Warts can heal themselves or spread. They occasionally cause pain or break down and form sores. They can be removed by chemical or surgical means.

Scabies is caused by a small mite which burrows into the skin and lays its eggs in the process. It causes a very irritating rash usually worse at night. The rash can be on the wrists, ankles, folds of the armpits or on the penis. Sleeping with somebody who has scabies is the commonest way of catching it.

Infection with lice causes 'crabs', which feed on skin and blood. One particular form of louse prefers to live in and on the pubic hair. It is crab-shaped (hence the name), about the size of a pin-head and greyish-green in colour. It lays its eggs on the hairs which then get matted together. The nits hatch out and start feeding by biting and blood sucking, thus causing the intense itching. They are spread by close bodily contact.

Chancroid (soft sore) and lymphogranuloma venereum (LGV) are both very rare in this country but do occur in the tropics. They could be acquired there by holiday makers or be brought here by immigrants.

The most recently discovered sexually transmitted disease is called hepatitis B. It is a virus infection which can lead to jaundice and in some cases chronic liver failure.

It is becoming more common amongst homosexuals and some men are chronic carriers. Although carriers suffer no symptoms they can remain infectious for years. There is, as yet, no cure. Some women have been infected by male carriers but there is no evidence yet that women are infecting men.

There are just two other conditions I would like to mention briefly. The first is the 'kissing disease', a popular name for glandular fever (infective mononucleosis). It has unjustifiably got this reputation of being spread by kissing. It is indeed spread by what doctors call 'droplet infection' via the saliva, but is not unique in this respect as a number of other infections can also be spread in this way, i.e., by close contact with saliva from coughing and sneezing as well as kissing.

The last condition is a much more serious one and that is cancer of the cervix (neck of the womb). This traditionally has been associated with sexual promiscuity. One argument for this association is its rarity in nuns and virgins. On the other hand there is an increased risk for those who have intercourse from an early age, a high frequency of intercourse, re-marry, have numerous pregnancies, more than one sex partner and sexually transmitted infections. The implication from these other associations is that it will increase. Early detection by cervical smears, complete abstinence or more frequent use of barrier methods of contraception could help to counter this.

To return to the more 'traditional' sexually transmitted diseases, is there anything that can be done to prevent further increases? On a personal level the most obvious advice is don't expose yourself to the risk. If you must, the condom (FL) affords some protection and so does thoroughly washing with soap and water (not antiseptics or disinfectants) and passing urine immediately after intercourse. But it's better to be safe than sorry, so the best course of action is to go for a medical check-up as soon as possible.

You can either go and see your own G.P. or refer yourself (you don't need a doctor's letter) to your local special clinic. The address can be got from your local hospital, public health department, posters in public lavatories or telephone directory. In some areas there is a special telephone number to ring for further information about V.D.

At the special clinic you will be treated in the strictest confidence and no one will moralize or preach at you. The most important way of trying to prevent further spread is by contact tracing, i.e., everyone you've recently slept with, which with your permission can be done in very discreet ways.

Other preventive measures have included better education and information for the general public. This has been a mixed blessing because it tends to foster self-diagnosis with the very dangerous implication that if you haven't got any symptoms you must be all right. This particularly applies to female cases who may be highly infectious to others yet have no outstanding symptoms.

At any of the big city clinics it is likely that between 20–30 per cent of the patients would be homosexual, so this is another aspect which requires further attention. For a fuller discussion of homosexuality see Chapter 9.

Prostitution is not considered to be an important reason for the recent increase in these diseases; immigrants and travellers probably are, and of course, there is that old standby, our 'permissive society', especially the younger generation's seemingly much more casual attitude towards sex. There are not yet any satisfactory immunization techniques.

There is still an immense fear of V.D. partly as a hang-over from the olden times when it was regarded as the 'wages of sin' but partly from the belief that it was incurable. As for the latter there has been effective treatment for syphilis since 1910 and for gonorrhoea since 1936.

As quacks and charlatans have always thrived on people's fear of V.D. and intense desire for secrecy, the Venereal Disease Act of 1917 was passed. This made it an offence, with severe penalties, for any unqualified person to give advice about V.D. or to advertise any such service. Nowadays at an average special clinic only about 25 per cent of patients attending will have legally defined V.D. Don't worry about not having it, wasting everybody's time or seeming to create a fuss about nothing, it is all part of a doctor's job to diagnose, explain, reassure, advise and where appropriate give specific treatment.

9

Coming Out

'Coming out' means admitting to yourself and to others that you are homosexual. The word itself is derived from 'homos' meaning 'same' (and not the Latin for man) and is used to describe sexual attraction of a man for a man or a woman for a woman. There is no special name for male homosexuality but the female variety is variously called lesbianism, sapphism or tribadism. The first two are derived from Lesbos, the Greek island in the Aegean where lived the poetess Sappho. She was born about 612 B.C. and ran a kind of female literary society. Tribadism should only be used for a particular sexual practice (from the Greek 'to rub'). There are many popular terms in use as well, the most generally accepted one now being 'gay'.

The essential part of any definition is a definite preferential erotic attraction to a member of the same sex. This usually, but not inevitably, also involves some physical expression of this attraction. When this is so we can talk about homosexual behaviour or a person being a practising homosexual.

But just because you indulge in homosexual behaviour does not necessarily mean you're homosexual; some can take it or leave it or only indulge under very special conditions like being shut up in a single sex community, as in prison.

That homosexuality is a matter of degree and not a simple 'black or white' distinction, was emphasized by Kinsey and co-workers, who devised a rating scale which has been used in research. It is a seven point scale, so that if you are exclusively heterosexual you score 0, if exclusively homosexual 6 and if equally homosexual and heterosexual (bisexual) you score 3. There are a further two intermediary grades on both the heterosexual side (1 and 2) and homosexual side (4 and 5).

It is very difficult to give a reliable estimate as to just how many homosexuals there are in the community but a reasonable guess would be for those who are entirely and persistently homosexual about 1 in 25 of the adult male population and 1 in 45 of the female.

It is relatively rare to be equally bisexual (Kinsey 3) but certainly a proportion (it is impossible to give a precise figure) of homosexuals do marry and have children. A famous example was Oscar Wilde. Probably more lesbians than male homosexuals marry as it is easier for a woman to adapt, not only to intercourse but to married life in general. This has the added advantage of satisfying parents and society in general, as well as giving her the children she may want, along with long term security.

Occasionally a lesbian teams up with a male homosexual in a sort of unconsummated marriage with both independently continuing with their own sex lives. A very rare combination with seldom lasts very long, is called troilism, in which a bisexual person lives with both homosexual and heterosexual partners at the same time.

But it cannot be stressed too often that it is useless and potentially harmful to all concerned to simply advise a young homosexual either that it's just a passing phase and he'll grow out of it or to 'find yourself a woman', get married or have a baby.

The general public is still very ignorant about homosexuality. For instance, many still believe that all male homosexuals are effeminate, like to dress up in female clothes and generally 'ape' women. A few extreme and notorious examples get all the publicity so it's assumed that they must all be like this. They're not, with the majority being indistinguishable from the rest of the population.

They cannot either be neatly divided into active and passive nor the women into 'fem' and 'butch'. There are, too, plenty of men who are quiet, sensitive, artistic, even somewhat effeminate, who are nevertheless entirely heterosexual. Likewise there are tough guy, rugby playing types, who to all outward appearances are very masculine indeed, yet are homosexual.

So you cannot recognize the average homosexual by his dress or manner, nor, incidentally, can they readily recognize each other. Another common mistake is to equate all homosexuals with child molesters or paedophiliacs (men sexually attracted to prepubertal children); nor do homosexuals 'degenerate' into this. Most homosexuals, as do most heterosexuals, prefer somebody roughly their own age.

A related condition, made popular by psychoanalysis but again frequently misunderstood, is latent or repressed homosexuality. It is suggested that deep down in all of us there are homosexual urges which are kept at bay by powerful forces so that they are not consciously recognized. What is confused here is the difference between having the potential to respond in a homosexual way and a fully-fledged homosexual pattern simply lying dormant.

It is in any case a difficult thing to prove and because of this it has been used to 'explain' other sexual problems, e.g., impotence or orgasmic dysfunction. At a more superficial level men who don't marry and appear rather passive and effeminate can be accused of being latent homosexuals. But on the other hand so can the man who is always chasing after women on the basis he's trying to prove to himself and to others he's a 'real' man. So you can't win with this sort of theory!

The big question is, why you become a homosexual in the first place, are you born that way or made into one by certain early experiences? The simple answer is that in spite of a lot of research, we still don't know for sure.

It is a complicated matter with various possible combinations of different causes. If the condition is truly hereditary then it should be present in some other members of your family. Technically this is very difficult to investigate but even if true it would soon die out as relatively few homosexuals do marry and have children. Twin studies are also inconclusive.

An older theory was that a homosexual was 'really' a member of the opposite sex or even an intermediate sex. This has now been conclusively disproved as homosexuals have normal sex chromosomes, i.e., a male homosexual is XY.

Another theory is that there is something wrong in the balance between the male (androgens) and female (oestrogens) sex hormones or possibly some fault 'higher up' in the overall control mechanism. However, it seems that these hormones only affect the strength of your sexual feelings (libido) but not its direction. The embryonic brain at a critical stage in development can also be affected by circulating sex hormones, especially androgens. The brain may then get 'primed' with possible future consequences for sexual behaviour.

But much of this work is based on animal experiments which cannot be uncritically accepted as giving us the answers to the vastly more complicated human situation.

The early influence of your parents, especially your mother is probably much more important than your hormones although, of course, you can have both or several different factors all operating together. A typical background for a male homosexual is a distant, unsympathetic father and a overpossessive and seductive mother. He is often described as a 'mother's boy'. He may also be the last born of a relatively old mother. One parent families could be especially at risk.

A lesbian may have had special difficulties with her father, who seemed to her to have been weak, ineffectual or cruel. Her mother, too, may have had her own problems, so that she presents a poor model for the girl to copy. Whatever the precise combination there is invariably some difficulty in admiring and wanting to be like the same sex parent. The Freudian explanation is based on a faulty handling of the Oedipus Complex.

Another fairly common family background factor is a puritanical attitude towards sex. This either goes by default as being unmentionable or is presented as entirely nasty and animal. The most modern theories emphasize hidden crippling fears of the opposite sex, which like 'bad habits' have been learnt in earlier life.

Actually early signs of homosexuality are difficult to detect. Schoolboy or girl 'crushes', tomboy or cissy behaviour are not reliable guides to future homosexuality. A number of shy, sensitive adolescents do develop very intense and passionate friendships with a member of the same sex or become terribly interested in and idolize some popstar, to the extent that they themselves begin to worry in case they are homosexual. They usually aren't and are just unsure of themselves. They admire and envy what the other person seems to stand for rather than the person himself, like popularity, success, social ease, fame and so on.

On the other hand, 'true' homosexual feelings often do start to emerge in adolescence with a feeling of being different from the others. This can lead to great anxiety and even panic. If this is also coupled with a strong sex drive (normal at this age) he may not know quite literally what to do with himself. Homosexual acts are still illegal at this age and he may be in a great quandary about telling his parents. He may have nobody he can sufficiently trust to talk to about his feelings.

What do not seem to be important causative factors are attempts at early seduction or early sexual shocks. For example a single instance of a young boy being fondled or masturbated by an older man, if dealt with sensibly, need have no lasting ill effects. Likewise there are very few girls who do not witness at least one act of 'indecent exposure' but this does not put them off men for life or turn them into lesbians.

Perhaps more prolonged contact with a practising homosexual could 'tip the balance' if the youngster was already predisposed to react in this way. This is one reason why the law makes a distinction between homosexual and heterosexual age of consent, on the grounds that a young adolescent who is still unsure of himself, sexually and otherwise, should be protected from undue influence.

The present legal position is governed by the Sexual Offences Act 1967, which does not apply to Scotland, Northern Ireland, The Armed Forces or the merchant navy. This amends the 1956 Act under which prosecutions can still take place. The present Act stipulates that it is no longer an offence for two adult homosexuals (over age 21, not 18) to indulge in anal intercourse or other sexual acts which can come under the legal definition of 'gross indecency', as long as it's done in private and they both consent. If charges are to be brought it must be with the approval of the Director of Public Prosecutions and proceedings must be instituted within a year of committing the alleged offence. Penalties vary up to a maximum of ten years' imprisonment.

Lesbians are let off and the only time legislation was introduced (in 1921) to try and make 'gross indecency' apply to two females, it was turned down by the House of Lords. So this is sex discrimination in reverse and one area where females have always been better treated— if you can call being ignored better treatment. One other discriminatory aspect is not so well known. We have just noted that anal intercourse is now permitted between two adult consenting homosexuals but it is not between consenting heterosexuals. In theory a man having anal intercourse with his wife can be prosecuted and receive anything up to life imprisonment. Clearly our sexual laws are again in need of some radical revisions.

It is interesting, though, to compare male and female homosexuals when they are seen to retain characteristics typical of their own sex. For instance male homosexuals are more promiscuous, have fewer lasting relationships, have male prostitutes, are aroused by a greater number of stimuli and so on.

For a lesbian a problem can be that she still retains a normal maternal instinct and may desperately want a child. It has recently been queried in the courts whether a lesbian could make a suitable mother. This can arise, for instance, in divorce proceedings when the custody of the children is decided. Also whether or not a lesbian couple should be allowed to adopt a child. Recently some lesbian couples have got round this by one of them getting pregnant by means of artificial insemination (AID).

These questions, raised by society at large, really hinge on the notion as to whether you can be 'abnormal' in your sex life yet 'normal' in every other respect. Some people would argue that the various background factors already mentioned would produce neurotic or otherwise unbalanced homosexuals, and could equally well be found in psychiatric patients in general and even many delinquents. In other words they are non-specific. There is some truth in this, particularly as so much of the research has been done on homosexuals who have come for help or treatment.

What really wants doing is to select very different types of parents and then follow them up for many years to see not just what sort of children they produce but what sort of adults. This avoids the bias of arguing backwards from a selected group of adult homosexuals going largely on what they say their parents and upbringing was like. You would also have to try and explain why one particular child grew up into a homosexual and not his brother or sister.

What is the relationship between homosexuality and mental disorder? Clearly homosexuality as such is not an illness but in some cases homosexual behaviour (as well as heterosexual) can be a symptom of a disturbed personality, a neurotic disorder or very occasionally a psychotic one. Much depends on who you are studying, how you define your terms and the methods used.

For example in one study I carried out on over a hundred lesbians I was very careful to get volunteers and not use patients. I found that 20 per cent had a previous psychiatric history and that standard psychological tests showed something like 50–60 per cent had average or normal scores.

Therefore there are a group of 'happy homosexuals', who have accepted their condition and are as well adjusted to it as a still largely hostile society will allow. To lump all homosexuals together as 'sick' perverts, degenerates or some other pseudo-scientific term is really only a way of saying you disapprove of them. On the other hand it's too simple just to say it's an alternative life-style—like living in a commune—something you consciously decide to be or do. You do not have to classify it as an illness to want to explain how it might come about.

Any minority group, especially when surrounded by

disapproval, tends to develop a 'ghetto mentality'. Typical characteristics are to become inward looking, insecure, oversensitive, lonely, guarded and with a large chip on the shoulder which in extreme cases can amount to a more frank persecutory (paranoid) attitude. Sometimes there is an over-compensation; a flaunting, a rather brittle arrogance, an air of superiority, of being 'special'. Under the circumstances it's natural to develop you own (gay) subculture.

However in the last decade there has been an increased tolerance and understanding of homosexuality. In America in the early 1950s homosexuals began to get together, initially for self-help but later to act as pressure groups for legal and social changes. These 'homophile' organizations later spread to England. In fact there is a bewildering and ever changing variety of them. Some are for lesbians only, others for both sexes. Special magazines are produced, counselling and befriending services are available as well as emergency telephone help rather on the lines of the Samaritans. Others still take up the political issues but may be counter-productive if too militant.

Life is still very difficult for homosexuals, particularly for those who want to live together like a married couple. It's easily forgotten that it's not just a sexual relationship; indeed for many lesbian couples it is more emotional with the sexual side being relatively unimportant. For some it's not really sexual at all—what they are really looking for is a mother substitute.

But couples have to live ordinary lives as well, so that when a lesbian is accused of being 'masculine', she very often has to be as there is no man around to do the traditionally masculine jobs. Similarly when male homosexuals are disparagingly depicted as acting like housewives.

The double standard again comes out when hetero-sexuals point out how male homosexuals are responsible for the recent increase in V.D., how promiscuity abounds; one night stands and sordid encounters in public lava-tories, male prostitutes and a trade in pornography. As if there were no female prostitutes, sordid sexual encounters and exploitation between men and women; or no great increase in gonorrhoea amongst young girls and so on. The prejudice is also seen in our society's reaction to a broken love affair. Everyone sympathizes with a jilted lover—as long as he's heterosexual!

The Churches have also a very bad record of intolerance towards homosexuals although this is now slowly changing. There has recently been formed a Gay Christian Movement, an inter-denominational group for committed Christians who are also homosexual.

But such emotive phrases as 'unnatural' vice, crimes or sins against nature are still being used, without it being at all clear what is really meant. Presumably against the natural order of things. But homosexual behaviour is widespread amongst animals. So in this sense it's more natural than unnatural. Although this argument can be taken too far and be turned round the other way and called 'animal' in a disparaging way. The narrowist view of all is to regard all sexual behaviour that cannot lead to preg-nancy as unnatural.

To sum up. It is often a lonely, difficult and unhappy life, particularly in old age. But homosexuals do seem to make a large contribution to the arts and creative pro-fessions and hence enrich all our lives. Homosexuality may also lead to a reduction in male aggression and delin-quency. For the individual, possible benefits are freedom from family ties and worries, more money and the pros-pect of a gayer (in all senses) life, freer and more spon-taneous.

Recent reforms demanded by some pressure groups include equality with heterosexuals, no more no less, which would mean the same age of consent, some form of marriage contract, easier adoption of children, the right to express themselves in public and to be treated as true 'next of kin'.

10

Coming Differently

To some, the sort of sexual behaviour described in this chapter is perverted, 'kinky', sick or just plain revolting and certainly should not be permitted by law. In order to get away from this hothouse atmosphere a more neutral term is needed; this is why 'deviant' was introduced, although it can be used in different ways. It is best used in the sense of unusual, uncommon or different from the average but not necessarily sick or wrong, even though certain sections of society may well disapprove.

Religious influences have always been important in trying to curb any sexual experimentation, to keep you on the 'straight and narrow'. It is no coincidence that the 'normal' position for intercourse—man on top of woman —is called the missionary position.

But what is considered normal behaviour in one society or indeed in our own society at different times, varies enormously. In one survey of 76 societies from all over the world homosexual activities were considered normal and socially acceptable for certain members of the community by 64 per cent. In general it was found that homo-sexuality was more often found in the more restrictive communities, where sexual behaviour was subject to formal rules.

One other aspect of the 'abnormality' of deviant sex is when this particular outlet becomes the only or sole way of expressing your sexuality. In other words, if you can only obtain an orgasm by being tied up and whipped, then there is surely something wrong.

Most deviant sex is indulged in by males; why this should be so is not clear. How much is biologically or innately determined and how much by social and cultural factors is open to argument. But there is much more variation in men anyway (e.g., in intelligence), they are more easily sexually aroused, particularly visually, and seem to need more variety in their sexual outlets.

Nevertheless social factors are important and this is one of the spheres where women come off best. For example, if a man walks down the High Street dressed like a woman, he's likely to be arrested and then sent for a psychiatric opinion. If a woman walks down the High Street dressed like a man, it is called fashionable, everybody is very indulgent and she gets away with it.

Part of the prejudice against homosexuals is their indulgence in 'unnatural practices', such as anal intercourse. But many people do not realize that (as one survey showed) about 20 per cent of all married couples indulge in it at some time as well. Also the terms used have a very muddled history and are still a source of confusion. Buggery and sodomy have been used to describe homosexual acts, heterosexual acts, anal intercourse with a boy (paederasty) or sexual acts with an animal (bestiality).

According to the Bible, the city of Sodom was to be destroyed because of its inhabitants' wickedness. When it was pointed out that total destruction would also kill the innocent, two angels were sent to find some virtuous men. Whilst in Lot's house, the male inhabitants of the city crowded round and demanded his guests be brought out so that they might 'know them'. The Hebrew word used can be interpreted either in a sexual sense or in a more general one of 'become acquainted with'. But in the story Lot offered his two daughters instead. When the crowd persisted in their demands they were struck blind.

Modern scholarship has shown the whole story to be a

hodge-podge, with later additions and interpretations, including references to male prostitution and bestiality. The most likely explanation is that the city was destroyed by an earthquake and this was seen as retribution for the far greater sins of pride, contentment, ignoring the needy and possibly some general sexual promiscuity. It's only much later in history that homosexuality was dragged into it.

The origin of the name 'bugger' illustrates how sexually and socially deviant behaviour became equated. Also how any 'way-out' group which offends the Establishment, religious or otherwise, tends to have further accusations of sexual irregularities made against it. In its strict origin buggery did not refer to a deviant sexual practice at all but to a group of heretical religious sects (Albigensians) in the 12th–13th centuries, who were thought to have originated in Bulgaria; 'bugger' then became a corruption of 'Bulgar'. So next time you call somebody a sod or a bugger, watch what you're saying!

Bestiality, in the sense of actually having sexual intercourse with an animal as a preferred method of sexual outlet, is very rare, and practically confined to farm workers of limited intelligence. A favourite theme in pornography is a woman being 'raped' by an animal, thus degrading her even further by putting her on the same 'animal' level. But lesser degrees of sexual involvement with animals are not all that unusual, particularly with dogs (e.g., masturbating them, sleeping with them and teaching them to lick your genitals) and horses.

Transvestism, cross-dressing or dressing in 'drag' is another example of deviant sexual behaviour although there are several different types. It is a normal male heterosexual characteristic to be partly turned on by sexy female underwear, so that the sexually desirable woman and her bra and panties are very closely associated. It's only a short step from this to want to actually wear them yourself. Most men who do this are heterosexual and will often masturbate to orgasm when so attired. The clothes themselves give immediate sexual gratification and act as a fetish. This does not occur with women and they may find it hard to understand.

Occasionally female underwear is worn under a conventional shirt and pin-striped city suit. Many a wife has got a shock when she accidentally discovers her husband dressed up in her clothes. For some men this becomes a compulsion, which may then lead them to buy or steal female underwear.

Homosexuals may dress in 'full-drag' (the name possibly comes from a long dress dragging on the ground) in order to tempt other males to have sex with them. In this case they want to look as much like a woman as possible but don't necessarily get any immediate sexual pleasure from the clothes themselves. The more butch-type lesbian may also dress in complete male attire and adopt male mannerisms, because she feels more natural and comfortable like this.

Occasionally transvestism is part of a wider disorder in which the man believes he really is a woman. Then there are a whole group of professional entertainers who make their living from female impersonation. Our own traditional pantomime is a good example of mixed-up gender roles. There is, too, a long operatic tradition of breeches or trouser roles for female singers, sometimes being further complicated by the character already being played by a female rather than a male pretending to be a female (e.g., Octavian in *Der Rosenkavalier*). In the much rarer instances when men play female roles it is always in a comic capacity—and never to be taken seriously. Of course the librettists and composers are all male!

Another reason for this difference is that for women to

want to imitate 'superior' men was all right and under-standable but there must be something very wrong with a man wanting to be an inferior female. This is shown too, in an interesting tradition of female transvestite saints, such as Joan of Arc and several others, but no male ones.

One famous historical example of male transvestism was the Chevalier d'Eon de Beaumont (1728–1810). He was a distinguished diplomat in the service of Louis XV and spent forty-nine years as a man and thirty-four as a woman. It was from his name that Havelock Ellis wanted to call the condition eonism and also that of a self-help group for heterosexual transvestites which calls itself The Beaumont Society.

Transsexualism was the term coined in 1949 to describe individuals who wanted to change their sex. Such a man has a gender identity problem and may firmly believe, in spite of all evidence to the contrary, that he is really a female trapped in a male body. In spite of the fact that most small girls at some time in their lives want to be boys and what has already been said about 'inferior' woman, transsexualism is very rare in women.

In fact, it's impossible to change your sex and all trans-sexuals have normal sex chromosomes, so that a male wanting a 'change of sex' operation will have XY chromo-somes. This is recognized in law so that whatever operation a male (XY) has he cannot get married as a woman. There are many well publicised sex changes, the latest being Jan Morris who wrote 'her' autobiography describing what it feels like, under the title *Conundrum*.

What you really end up as is a castrated and mutilated male, even though superficially, with the aid of plastic surgery and oestrogens, an outwardly female appearance. Some of these cases aren't strictly sexual at all. I have seen a number of men who feel inadequate as men and think it's a soft option to become a female in the mistaken belief that they can then be totally passive and cared for by others.

Fetishism, strictly speaking, means obtaining sexual pleasure from inanimate objects, like clothes. The object is closely linked with a sexually desired person but it is the thing or a particular part of the woman and not the woman herself which turns on the fetishist. Common objects are hair, rubber and plastic macs, the foot, shoes and boots, leather and silk articles. Both smell and feel can be important elements. In a way it's an extension of treating a woman as a sex object—tits, bum or legs—and simply being excited by these. Occasionally rather unusual characteristics like a squint, serve the same purpose.

Let us now look at sexual behaviour that involves violent or aggressive behaviour, whether giving it or receiving it. 'You always hurt the one you love' in the words of one popular song. Again terms are often used very loosely.

Sadism or being sadistic means getting sexual pleasure or 'kicks' out of harming others, either physically or by humiliating them. The sexual significance of sadistic wishes or behaviour may be obvious, or hidden and much more subtle. In most men it's only sadistic daydreams or fantasies that are indulged in, these are very common, but are never put into practice.

The name is derived from the Marquis de Sade (1740–1814) who had the rather curious notion that because a woman's sensation of pleasure in sex could be shammed but pain could not, pain rather than pleasure was the highest form of sexual activity. Because of various rather half-hearted attempts to put this theory into practice he spent nearly twenty years of his life in prison. During this time he wrote the many notorious novels for which he is best known. They mostly consist of a peculiar mixture of turgid philosophizing and rather morbid sadistic fantasies.

Hurtful behaviour varies all the way from innocent 'love bites' to lust murder, gentle erotic stroking, pinching and bottom spanking to outright flagellation (whipping). This last is held to be a particularly English deviation, often blamed on our public schools with their long tradition of corporal punishment. There is, as well, the element of humiliating the victim, even though in some cases he is more than willing.

The counterpart to sadism is masochism—the sexual pleasure gained from being at the receiving end. It can be consciously sought as in flagellation or unconsciously arranged or invited. Sometimes it has the further implication of seeking punishment to overcome a sense of guilt. This would seem to be a universal human potential.

The name is derived from a literary gentleman, Leopold von Sacher-Masoch (1836–95), who held that women had been created to subdue men's animal passions. Eventually all his novels contained scenes of a man being whipped by a commanding and dominating woman. Because he himself was a fur-fetishist, the woman doing the whipping was also dressed in furs. His best known novel is called *Venus in Furs*. Another variant of this is 'bondage', which involves being made totally helpless by being tied up and then perhaps being beaten or masturbated.

Inflicting sexually stimulating harm on yourself again varies enormously from rather rough self-masturbation using various objects (I once had a female patient who used a milk bottle and a male a vacuum cleaner) to inserting things up the urethra or rectum. Surgeons are sometimes called on to remove the most unlikely objects from either bladder or bowel. Other very dangerous practices are half strangling or suffocating yourself or giving electric shocks to your genitals.

Frottage or frotteurism will be familiar to most women

who regularly travel on London's underground trains. It refers to obtaining sexual pleasure by rubbing up against another person's body. Men may press themselves up against a woman's bottom or surreptitiously feel her breasts with an elbow.

Rape used to be defined as 'unlawful carnal knowledge of a woman without her consent, by force, fear or fraud' and is another obvious example of sexual violence, at least in some cases. But note that it was, and still is under the new law, without her consent, and not necessarily by force. Closely related offences are attempted rape and indecent assault.

Rape has attracted a lot of attention in recent years and the law has been changed by the Sexual Offences (Amendment) Act, 1976. So that now the names of the victim as well as of the alleged ravisher, if innocent, are no longer published. Also it helps to clarify the point as to whether or not a man really believed the woman was consenting or just pretending and playing 'hard to get'. It also protects the woman from intensive questioning about her sex life. This law does not apply to married couples.

Actually 'rape' includes many different acts and situations. From two lovers out for a drink and indulging in heavy petting afterwards when the man gets 'carried away', has intercourse and is later had up for rape, to the most abnormally aggressive sadistic psychopath who rapes and then murders his victim.

A certain proportion of rapes (in one recent survey 66 per cent) are not really sexual at all but simply aggressive assaults carried out by a man with a history of other types of violence. He may also be an alcoholic and even impotent. It is by no means always the 'sex maniac' full of uncontrollable lust, as popularly supposed. At most, this type wants to frighten, humiliate and degrade the woman, certainly not to give her any sexual pleasure or even get any himself.

Another popular (mainly male) idea is that all women really want to be raped or at best could always avoid it if they really wished. This is a travesty of the truth. The 'lie back and enjoy it' school know very little about what it can be like—terrifying, sordid, painful and humiliating. It is also a very different matter from a woman wishing that somebody she loved would show a little more ardour and forcefulness in his love making. There is too, still a hang-over from psychoanalysis and Freud's very poor view of women; that they were by nature excessively passive and masochistic.

The apparent recent increase in rape (e.g., 1,100 cases reported to the police in 1976 compared with 422 in 1963) has been blamed on many things, but often on porn-ography, without ever considering other possibilities. The incidence of sexual crimes can be artificially increased or decreased simply by a change in police policy, a change in the law or public attitudes. Women generally are now more militant and perhaps what is happening is that more of them are reporting rape, particularly if their names will no longer be mentioned.

There are other types of rape which are not so well known to the general public. For example paedophiliac rapists, who attack girls aged 14 or less (49 per cent in the survey already mentioned) and sometimes elderly women as well (gerontophilia). Some of these rapists say that an absence of pubic hair specifically arouses them or the fact that the victims are physically weak.

There is also group rape (or 'gang-bang') often per-petrated by a group of adolescent boys on a younger adolescent girl. Incidentally boys under 14 are held, in law, to be incapable of committing rape. Finally there is homo-sexual rape.

Allied to those offences is 'oral' aggression or wanting to shock, hurt or humiliate by means of words, for instance, using obscene or filthy language (coprolalia). There is one very rare disease in which the unfortunate patient not only has multiple involuntary twitches but also utters grunting and barking noises as well as having to shout obscenities.

The man who makes obscene telephone calls is another example of deviant behaviour. As he receives his sexual pleasure from this, it is perhaps better classified under fetishism. It is more common than is realized particularly amongst pre-adolescent and adolescent boys. Women victims are chosen at random from the telephone directory. The caller may masturbate in response to the woman's outraged reaction. Occasionally this form of sexual release becomes a true compulsion. The way to stop it happening to you again is not to be shocked or excited but to reply in a quiet manner and suggest that he should have some treatment.

The indecent exposer ('flasher') or exhibitionist, as defined by the law, is again male. (Women are actually encouraged to expose themselves and even get paid for it in strip-tease.) It is rather quaintly worded: 'Anyone who wilfully and indecently exposes his person, whether in private, or in public, with intent to insult a female...'. The men who do this sort of thing are mostly rather passive, inoffensive characters, who do not 'progress' to rape or other more serious offences. The exposure, usually to a strange girl under the age of puberty, is an end in itself. He may or may not have an erection or masturbate himself. Some are truly compulsive and return to the same spot and are easily caught.

Somewhat akin to this is voyeurism or scopophilia—the strong desire to look at couples making love, women undressing, or their genitals, or occasionally when urinating or defaecating. A synonym for this is 'peeping Tom' which is derived from the seventeenth-century addition to the Lady Godiva legend. The sexual pleasure of watching or listening to a woman urinating was called undinism by Havelock Ellis, who admitted getting pleasure out of it himself.

Other excretory interests, such as a desire to drink urine or to eat faeces (coprophagia) are usually associated with some mental disorder. So too are vampirism (the desire to drink blood), cannibalism and wanting to have sexual intercourse with a corpse (necrophilia).

Most societies studied seem to have some taboos on certain closely related individuals having intercourse with each other. If they do it's called incest. Interestingly, incest was not made a criminal offence in England until 1908. The prohibited degrees of relationship stem from the Bible (Leviticus 18) somewhat modified and now incorporated into the Sexual Offences Act, 1956. A man may not have intercourse with his mother, sister, half-sister, daughter or granddaughter or a woman with her father, brother, half-brother, son or grandfather.

It is the blood relationships which give rise to the offence, so that step-relatives are excluded. The most commonly encountered forms of incest are father–daughter and brother–sister and are more frequent than is realized. Incest is very much affected by intelligence as well as social and cultural factors and is not necessarily associated with any gross abnormality. That children born from incestuous unions can be perfectly normal is attested to by the fact that it was the norm for certain royal families in ancient times e.g., in Egypt. Cleopatra, one of the most beautiful women of all time was the product of many incestuous marriages and herself married her own brother.

Group sex, sometimes referred to as 'wife swapping' (but never husband swapping!) lies behind such advertisements as 'Young swinging couple desire to meet similar'. This is the sort of thing you are always reading about but never seem to actually come across in ordinary everyday life. This is, perhaps, because most normal people would still prefer to have their sex in private. This is not to be confused with a 'groupie', who is a young girl prostitute living with a male pop group.

A lot could be said on the subject of prostitution, but I haven't the space to go into all the different varieties, heterosexual, homosexual, child, and so on. The most common has always been female prostitutes for men (very rare is the gigolo or hired man for a woman) and they undoubtedly perform a useful social service in spite of our society's continuing hypocritical attitude.

Some of the reasons why a man goes to a prostitute are to obtain relief from sexual tension when his wife or girl-friend is ill, absent or pregnant or when he's in a big city for only a relatively short time. He may want sex without commitment because he's so emotionally involved with his wife. Or he may want to experiment with a variety of sexual experiences. A young man may want to learn about sexual intercourse without seeming a novice in front of his girlfriend or be too shy to find a girlfriend of his own.

For the old, ugly or deformed a prostitute may be the only outlet; also for a man experiencing sexual difficulties or if he wants to indulge in some sexually deviant behaviour.

11

Coming for Treatment

By way of summary, before discussing specific ways of getting help and what forms of treatment are available, let me just list some of the main causes of sexual problems. For some people there will be a combination of several causes.

A. Immediate Causes
    1. Ineffectual sexual behaviour
    2. Fear of failure
    3. Personal and intellectual hang-ups
    4. Failure to communicate
    5. The actual situation

B. Background Causes
    1. Inner conflicts
    2. Social and cultural

C. Relationship Problems
    1. Marital discord
    2. Partner rejection
    3. No partner

D. Learned Causes

E. Physical Causes
    1. General or localized physical illness or disorder
    2. Physical handicaps
    3. Drugs, prescribed or non-prescribed
    4. Ageing

F. Mental Causes
    1. Severe neurotic illness
    2. Depression

3. Physical disorder of the brain
4. Mental handicap
5. Psychotic illness
6. Severe personality disorder.

There is no more vulnerable person than somebody with a sex problem, so do be careful in case you are exploited by unscrupulous people who are only after your money. As you must have realized by now many sex problems are complicated, have multiple interlocking causes, and do not lend themselves to instant 'magic' cures. This is not to say you can't be helped or indeed, can't do anything to help yourself.

Just because a clinic or centre has a posh name and a London address it does not mean that the people running it are properly qualified or know what they're doing. Small ads may promise you all sorts of things—pills, ointments, mechanical aids, hypnosis—but in most cases it's far wiser, in the first instance, to see your own doctor for a check-up and a talk about your problems.

There are a number of magazines available, the best known being *Forum*, to which you can write in confidence for further information and advice about your problems. If you wish to meet others with a similar sexual outlook, either for companionship, help or counselling, there are a number of 'self-help' organizations to meet your needs, e.g., for homosexuals and (heterosexual) transvestites.

Most big cities now have a number of 'sex-shops' or similar establishments often with a mail order business as well, which sell sexual aids of various sorts. They also sell sexy films, books and magazines, which may aid those with waning sexual interest. There is also a host of 'specialist' magazines for both male and female homosexuals, fetishists, sado-masochists and others.

There is no proven basis for any of the 'rejuvenation'

treatments, whether by injection of anti-sera, 'monkey glands' or vitamin preparations. You may see Vitamin E advertised. You get quite sufficient in an ordinary diet. Because gross deficiency causes sterility in rats does not mean it has any effect on human sexuality and reproduction—it doesn't.

Hormones can be applied externally (rubbed into the skin), given by mouth or by injection. Hormone cream as a bust developer does not work, nor will it increase the size of the penis. Injections and pills should only be given under medical supervision.

So-called aphrodisiacs should be avoided. Many preparations may appear to work, at least for a time, by what is called the placebo effect. This refers to the non-specific effects of a drug or the power of a totally inert substance to produce effects. In other words if you have high hopes and expectations, have faith in it and already believe it's going to work, it probably will at least at first. But it won't last.

Expensive price, 'testimonials' to its power (the sort doctors use or recommend), hints of exotic or oriental origins, impressive packaging, shape, colour and nasty taste all help to influence you. Highly suggestible people can even get 'side-effects', like a headache, from a placebo. Many 'tonics', vitamin and hormone preparations, herbal and nature cures, aphrodisiacs and even 'scientifically' designed or approved treatments fall into this category.

What about mechanical sex aids? There is a whole range of products designed to help with various sex problems but they are not available on prescription on the NHS. Some of them may help to boost a flagging sex life or just be good fun, but have certain disadvantages: first, that by using them you are not doing anything to understand what caused the problem and secondly, you may become dependent on them.

There are various 'rings' and other devices designed to go round the penis, to improve erections and help overcome impotence. The best known and the one which has undergone some medical trials is the Blakoe Energizing Ring. In addition to the mechanical support it also produces a tiny electrical current (not by batteries but by interaction with body sweat). Another smaller latex rubber device exerts pressure at the root of the penis and may help premature ejaculation.

There is also a vacuum penis developer (Chartham Method) whereby the penis is inserted into a tube, from which air is then withdrawn by means of a suction bulb. This can certainly produce an erection but it is doubtful —even if this was desirable—if it would produce any permanent increase in penis size.

Also available are all manner of penile prosthetics (substitutes) as well as supports for cases of partial or total impotence. There are three principle types of artificial penis; hollow with harness, solid with harness, and hand-held or dildo type. The hollow sort, into which the penis is inserted, also acts as a contraceptive sheath. A lubricating jelly is usually used with them.

Then there are the stimulant or 'personal' vibrators (one rather charmingly called the 'non-doctor' vibrator). These are usually phallic shaped, about the size of a small hand torch, made of plastic and containing batteries (some are mains operated). They can be embarrassingly noisy. There are various interchangeable 'ends' depending on whether you want to massage your face, penis, clitoris or insert it into your vagina. It can sometimes help a woman to experience orgasm for the first time. If too strong when directly put on the clitoral area, you can use your finger and then apply the vibrator to it. Vibrators should never be used in the bath as this could be dangerous. For extra hygiene, if it's going to be used inside the vagina, a condom can be used to cover the end.

There are a large number of other types of clitoral stimulators, which can be divided into two basic models. First, air filled latex penile rings with forward facing air filled projectors at right angles to the ring and secondly, latex penile sleeves or rings with solid forward facing pro-filed projectors set at right angles. There is also one for fitting on a finger.

A pelvic muscle exerciser (popularly known as a Geisha Ball) is a weighted latex rubber cylinder which is inserted into the vagina, like a tampon, where it rolls about causing some contraction of surrounding muscles and a pleasant sensation. More conventional ways of contracting the muscles around the vagina and the pelvic floor can be learnt (you can feel them contract by pretending or actually stopping the flow of urine, although you should always go on to completely empty your bladder). Strengthening these muscles may be useful after childbirth and contract-ing them during intercourse may add to the pleasure.

The more things that you stuff into the vagina the more chance there is of causing minor injuries as well as intro-ducing infection. They will also have to be taken out for intercourse and during menstruation.

Do not bother with so-called bust developers. There are various contraptions on the market involving suction cups and water. What these and other recommended exercises do is to develop the (pectoral) muscles, which lie behind the breast tissue, but do not directly affect the shape or firmness of the breasts themselves.

Other places where you can yourself seek help, par-ticularly if your marriage is in difficulties, are the Marriage Guidance Council or Family Planning Clinic. One approach used by many counsellors, you can try your-selves. This is the principle of 'give to get' or contract marital therapy. You can draw up a list of what you most like and dislike about your partner and then compare notes. You then agree on a first contract; if, for example, your husband will be more loving and demonstrative towards you, you in return will be more sexy and more active in initiating love play.

Treatment will normally be organized by your own doctor, who is also the best person to advise about private treatment if this is what you want. There are a number of clinics run by psychologists, who, in spite of calling themselves 'doctor' (by virtue of having a Ph.D.), are not medically qualified but nonetheless may be well qualified in certain psychological or behavioural techniques. In areas where there is a teaching hospital with university departments, there will be facilities for dealing with most sexual problems. Sometimes special clinics (other than V.D.) are called psychosexual, conjoint, marital or some such name. Different combinations of doctors and other workers man them, including psychiatrist, psychologist, gynaecologist, social worker and sometimes G.P. as well. Again your own doctor will know about those facilities available under the NHS and will arrange for you to go to one, with a letter of introduction.

Treatment methods available can be briefly summarized under three headings (not mutually exclusive and often combined): 1. Medical—such as drugs and hormones; 2. Surgical; 3. Psychological—various types of psychotherapy and behaviour therapy.

Hormone treatment should not be used indiscriminately, but only when a definite deficiency can be demonstrated. The levels of naturally occurring hormones in your body can now mostly be measured, either in blood or urine, although this is only available at some centres and can be costly and complicated. Male potency problems, provided there is a certain basic amount of testosterone present in the body, usually do not respond to

hormone treatment. When hormone deficiency does produce impotence it is usually through loss of sexual desire
and drive rather than through an inability to put desire
into action.

For damping down unacceptably strong sexual desires
in the male, oestrogens can be given, although this can in
effect produce a 'medical' castration as well as other
undesirable side-effects. Recently introduced are drugs
which counteract the effects of androgens (anti-
androgens); one such is called cyproterone acetate, and
is taken by mouth. But it does produce temporary
sterility by stopping sperm production.

It is very rare to be asked to treat excessive sexual
desire in a woman, for which there is little in the way of
hormone treatment except for trying various contraceptive
pills. Tranquillizers or other sedatives may be more
appropriate.

Contraceptive pills can also be used to treat some
menstrual disorders, particularly painful, heavy and
irregular periods. If ovulation is stopped, this usually
stops the pain as well. The pill can also be used to postpone
a period if it is important to do so (e.g., going abroad on
holiday) by taking the next course without a break. For
orgasmic difficulties hormones are of little use. Male sex
hormones should be used with extreme caution in women
as they can cause 'virilization', such as the growth of male
type hair and voice changes which can sometimes be
permanent.

When your sexual problems are closely bound up with
tension, anxiety or depression, tranquillizing and anti-
depressant drugs may be of great benefit, even though
they can themselves sometimes cause sexual difficulties.
The 'major' (more potent) tranquillizers may also cause
some loss of libido or problems with ejaculation.

Specific drugs, mainly antibiotics, are of course available for the treatment of the sexually transmitted diseases.

Surgical treatment may be necessary in certain cases of painful intercourse or when there is some physical impediment to successful intercourse, in either sex. Surgical castration for sexual problems is not practised in this country although it may have to be undertaken in a very few instances of serious disease.

An enlarged prostate gland can be cured by surgical intervention (prostatectomy); so common is this operation now that about 1 in 10 undergo it at some time in their lives. There are different methods of doing it, which should be discussed with your surgeon beforehand, as it can impair sexual function, both erectile and ejaculatory.

In women, sterilization, termination of pregnancy, some cases of sub-fertility and other gynaecological troubles may require surgical intervention. As a preliminary, a more minor procedure of a 'scrape' or D & C (dilatation and curettage), when the inside of the womb is scraped out, may be necessary. Hysterectomy (removal of the womb, having 'everything taken away', 'the' operation, etc.) may also be required, but usually the ovaries are left behind. It is not uncommon to get a bit depressed after this operation and even perhaps lose your sexual desire for a while.

Surgery for 'change of sex' operations is more controversial. It requires multiple operations, involving plastic surgery, along with large doses of sex hormones. It should not be undertaken without expert psychiatric assessment in the first place. Do not go privately to surgeons who are not properly qualified, either in this country or abroad. Other 'cosmetic' plastic surgery, simply to improve appearance or sex appeal, e.g., alter your bust, cannot be done on the NHS unless it is also in the interests of your general health.

Psychotherapy is the famous 'talking cure' and involves a

trained person deliberately establishing a professional relationship with you, with the object of removing or modifying existing symptoms and promoting positive personality growth. There are many different types of psychotherapy so that only the merest outline is possible here. It can vary from simple advice and counselling right the way through to psychoanalysis. Psychotherapy may be on an individual basis or with you and your partner together (conjoint or marital therapy) or in a larger group of about eight people.

Just talking to someone who has the time and the necessary training to listen to you and help you unburden yourself, in a friendly but confidential atmosphere and without censure or being shocked, can in itself be very helpful. You may feel you have terrible guilty secrets and all sorts of things you feel ashamed and mixed up about, which you have never been able to tell anybody before.

Counselling involves not only listening but also explanation, reassurance and practical advice. It may also involve putting you in touch with other helpful agencies or organizations, for example telling a homosexual about the various homophile organizations. For a more radical understanding of yourself and your problems, digging a little deeper may be necessary. This means going back over your childhood, development, relationship with your parents and so on. Fears, prejudices, wrong attitudes and mixed-up feelings can be sorted out. If necessary psychotherapy can be combined with other forms of treatment, such as taking special pills.

Psychotherapy is the best treatment for getting at inner conflicts and emotional hang-ups. Short-term psychotherapy—going on for weeks or months, as opposed to years—is available under the NHS and may involve regular visits (say one hour a week) to an out-patient clinic, arranged through your doctor. Psychoanalysis which involves much longer and more intense sessions, usually two or three a week for years, has to be obtained privately.

Behaviour therapy is concerned with altering behaviour by such means as correcting faulty habits which have been learned, combating anxiety and teaching new skills. It is this sort of approach which is usually referred to as 'sex therapy' and concentrated on the 'here and now' and the obvious problems rather than on any underlying conflicts.

There is though, a 'cart and horse' problem here: which came first, the marital tensions and personality problems of you and your partner, or your sex problems. In many ways it's so much easier to say, 'improve our sex life and the rest of the marriage will then be marvellous', when sometimes this is dodging the real issues. In other words some 'sex problems' are not really sex problems at all—they are just the tip of the iceberg—and it's the underlying causes which should be treated rather than the sexual problem as such. This needs to be worked out before embarking on a particular course of treatment.

Very generally it seems that conditions like vaginismus and premature ejaculation are more 'reflex' or mechanical disorders, which only secondarily cause other emotional and interpersonal problems, and hence respond best to treatment. All the others, in some degree or other are bound up with these other matters. But one very good reason why both partners should enter treatment (apart from the obvious situation when they both have sexual problems) is that treating only one could upset a very delicate balance. For example the partner may have been chosen in the first place because he was sexually non-demanding; if this is then altered on its own, after years of marriage, the other could react with a nervous break-down.

Some of the actual techniques used are relaxation

135

exercises, desensitization to specific fears, aversion therapy, stopping unwelcome thoughts, changing fantasies, learning how to assert yourself, specific sex techniques and many others. Again it is not possible to go into details but here are some brief examples, taking the easiest ones first.

With vaginismus it is important to eliminate any physical causes first. If there are none, then teaching relaxation and at the same time encouraging the woman to put into her vagina a series of (well lubricated) dilators of gradually increasing size, is usually very successful. When she has gained more confidence her husband can begin to insert the dilators himself. In this way she can prove to herself that something as big as an erect penis can easily be fitted into her vagina without pain or spasm.

The essential part of the treatment of premature ejaculation is to learn to postpone orgasm. A start can be made using self-masturbation, stopping just short of orgasm, waiting a few minutes and then starting again. This 'stop-start' technique is then used with your partner masturbating you. She stops immediately you signal approaching orgasm, waits a while and then goes on as before. Leading on from this—and this can be used straight away—is the 'squeeze technique'; this sounds rather painful but it isn't. Intercourse is banned until good control is obtained. His wife begins to masturbate him, as before, but just as orgasm is approaching squeezes the head of the penis by finger and thumb round the junction of the glans and shaft. Provided the timing is right, and this may require some practice as well as how precisely to hold the penis, ejaculation will not occur. The process can be repeated, with short pauses between stimulation, for up to 30–45 minutes.

With three weeks or so of daily practice most men become able to control ejaculation. When you both mutually decide to proceed to intercourse, this should be attempted with the female on top. Following several minutes stimulation and squeezing, she guides his penis into her vagina; both then lie quietly until he feels secure enough to begin gentle thrusting movements. Should he feel he's losing control, the penis should be withdrawn and the squeeze technique reapplied. When the situation has become controlled, intercourse can be resumed. This method also illustrates what I have previously stated, the need for a loving, co-operative partner.

Before going on to describe treatment methods in a bit more detail let us pause for a while to consider how these techniques were first used by Masters and Johnson.

As originally practised in America, a male and female therapist (preferably one medically qualified) took on a couple with sexual problems for an intensive two weeks' course. The couple lived together in a nearby hotel, away from home, children, family and business worries. Initially the female therapist took the history from the wife and the male therapist from the husband, a process which could take up to seven hours. A complete physical check-up was also undertaken. They then had a round table conference with the four of them, to plan further treatment. Much of the actual practice—the particular sexual tasks taught them—were then practised in the privacy of their hotel bedroom, with further joint sessions for reporting progress.

One of their basic tenets was that it was the 'relationship' itself that needed treatment, so a partner was necessary. In the early stages they did accept a few single patients for treatment and provided them with 'surrogate' partners, typically a woman for a single man and not the other way round. This practice they eventually abandoned and it cannot be recommended. There is only one centre in England that uses it.

The other main approach was to ban sexual intercourse until the couple had had a chance to get to know each other all over again, both psychologically and physically. Physically they are encouraged to touch, rub and massage each other—just to give pleasure—initially avoiding the genitals and breasts but later including all areas. This they called 'sensate focus'.

To illustrate, let us consider the treatment of a woman in her 40s with secondary orgasmic dysfunction. The partners are encouraged to think sexually and to communicate their desires to each other and to engage in genital sensate focus. The best position for this is for the husband to sit behind his wife, both totally nude, and with her sitting between his legs with her back towards him. This allows the best access to her breasts and genitals.

She is advised to guide her husband's hands to her erotic areas and to communicate clearly how and where she prefers to be stimulated. After a certain number of sessions desire becomes so intense that intercourse can no longer be postponed. At this point, following lengthy love-play, the wife adopts the superior position and guides her husband's penis into her, as he continues gentle stimulation of her body. When she feels ready she begins pelvic thrusting, which eventually culminates in a full orgasm or at least a very pleasurable experience.

The treatment of primary orgasmic dysfunction (never had an orgasm with sexual intercourse or under any circumstances) is rather more difficult. The main object is to overcome the inhibitory and excessive control which she has developed and which has prevented her orgasmic reflex from working. She is taught to focus on preliminary erotic sensations, learning to recognize and welcome them and not shut them off.

She may well also need to be distracted from thinking about her control, for instance by letting herself go mentally and indulging in whatever erotic fantasies she wants. This is frequently combined with psychotherapy to further understand any underlying conflicts and other factors which have made her so controlled. This combined approach of psychotherapy and learning particular mental and sexual techniques, may be all that is required.

For a very inhibited woman, who has never masturbated and never had an orgasm, the first steps may have to be to teach her how to masturbate and encourage her to overcome her inhibitions to do so. If she finds this difficult manually, then a vibrator may help. In this sort of case it's better to initially treat the woman on her own. When she has gained confidence and found that 'abandoning herself' is both very pleasant and not at all frightening, her husband can then be brought into it. Various joint techniques can then be tried until she eventually manages an orgasm during intercourse with her husband.

For the treatment of lack of erection similar techniques are adopted, in step-like sequence. An important aspect, here and elsewhere, is to give the patient permission to be 'selfish' and for the other partner to appreciate this. In other words until treatment is completed, to stop worrying about what effect their performance is having on their partner but simply to concentrate on their own pleasure. For failure to get or maintain an erection, treatment techniques would be a) sensate focus training; b) dispelling fear of failure; c) distracting obsessive thoughts; d) encouragement in being 'selfish'; e) coital techniques. For instance, taking advantage of a morning erection to have intercourse that very minute regardless of whether his wife is aroused or not.

For retarded ejaculation treatment can be by desensitization, like that for a phobia, only not done in imagination but in practice with his partner. First the factors inhibiting the patient must be identified and then gradually modified.

Favourite erotic fantasies and activities are used in the desensitizing procedures. Also find out under what circumstances he was able to successfully ejaculate in the past.

Many other examples and variations could be given. But as the M & J approach has had such world-wide publicity with increasing demands for similar treatment facilities to be made available here, it's worthwhile casting a critical eye on their published results. At the outset it's important to realize just what a highly selected group of people they were treating. They eliminated those with any physical or psychiatric abnormality. They were mostly intelligent (17.5 per cent medically qualified!), middle class, very well motivated, well off financially, and willing to spend a fortnight away from home. They also had two therapists, plenty of time and excellent facilities. Many had or were having psychotherapy as well.

Overall they had a 20 per cent failure rate, with a further 5 per cent relapse rate after a five year follow-up study. Best results were with vaginismus (no failures) and premature ejaculation (2.2 per cent failure rate). Erectile impotence did not do nearly so well—primary cases about 40 per cent failure and secondary about 26 per cent. Retarded ejaculation had a 40 per cent failure rate. The various types of orgasmic dysfunction had failure rates between 17–30 per cent. I have quoted the failure rates not because I want to emphasize this aspect, but because M & J do not always make clear what precisely they mean by 'cure' and 'improvement'. Also it should be noted that this was entirely uncontrolled; that is, there was no comparison with a similar group who had the same initial assessment but just had a two week holiday without any other specific treatment.

I'm not trying to 'knock' M & J, but simply want to help you get 'sex therapy' into perspective. Any doctor would welcome any well tried treatment to help his patients, but on the other hand, we don't want to raise false hopes. Variations of the M & J techniques are now being extensively used within the NHS without precisely following the original M & J approach, e.g., using only one therapist.

One recent English trial of different forms of treatment for erection failure divided patients into three groups: 1. had drug treatment for anxiety; 2. modified M & J programme; 3. no treatment. Results showed that neither drug treatment nor the M & J were in any way superior to no treatment. Whether patients recovered or not was related to various clinical factors rather than to what sort of treatment they received. Patients in whom impotence was caused by a specific psychological or physical upset did much better than those who had showed an insidious decline in sexual potency without any obvious causes.

Because of the shortage of suitably trained medical personnel, an experiment was initiated by the National Marriage Guidance Council to see if counsellors could become successful sex therapists in the M & J tradition.

Their estimate of about 50,000 couples needing help with sex problems is probably a gross underestimate. Many are still too shy or embarrassed to seek help.

The NMGC project involved 76 clients, 64 of whom assessed the results of their own treatment. Seven out of ten (70 per cent) reported a much improved sex life. Almost half said they were satisfied with treatment; 31 per cent expressed some disappointment and 3 per cent said they were worse. The treatment programme included sex films (as advocated by M & J) but did not accept the need for a male and female co-therapist for every couple.

In spite of denial by many behaviour therapists, a most important part of any treatment is not so much the precise sexual instructions, but your relationship with whoever is treating you. In many instances all that patients want is 'permission' from someone in authority and whom they respect to do their own thing and find their own level.

In case you have got the impression that only married couples are taken on for treatment I would like to make it clear that many young, single people, adolescents particularly, have sexual problems which can also be treated. Worry over homosexuality is an example. Many adolescents are so unsure of themselves that they do not even know whether they are just shy of the opposite sex or 'really' homosexual.

For those who are not exclusively homosexual and want to try and change more in the direction of heterosexuality, either psychotherapy or behaviour therapy can be useful forms of treatment. Indeed if the exclusively homosexual wants to become a better adjusted homosexual or has a particular sexual problem in his relationships, he too can be helped.

In some instances there may be a phobia or irrational fear of the opposite sex or even a particular aspect of a woman, like her pubic hair. John Ruskin, the nineteenth century art and social critic was repulsed by female pubic hair and his marriage had to be annulled. Most phobias can be treated by behaviour therapy, either by systematic desensitization or by creating some aversion to homosexuality and at the same time encouraging and rewarding interest in heterosexuality. Aversion therapy on its own is now seldom used, except for some cases of fetishism.

There is, though, an important ethical point in the treatment of any so-called deviant sexual behaviour. We have emphasized more than once throughout this book the great diversity in human sexual behaviour. Just because one section of society disapproves of some form of sexual behaviour, should this be 'treated', especially if the 'patient' is being coerced by others? In bygone times he might have been thought sinful rather than sick, and been dealt with by the ecclesiastical authorities, often very harshly. But are we being so very different, so very advanced, humanitarian and modern, by putting the doctor in the priest's place and making him society's agent for bringing the dissident into line? This is worth thinking about, particularly in the context of those patients who are more or less made to have treatment as part of some court order.

Appendix

SOME USEFUL NAMES AND ADDRESSES

THE BEAUMONT SOCIETY
BM Box 3084, London WC1V 6XX

For heterosexual transvestites.

BLAKOE LTD
225 Putney Bridge Road,
London SW15 2PY
(01–870 4251)

A reputable and long established firm who sell mechanical sexual aids and appliances by mail order.

BRENT CONSULTATION CENTRE
Johnston House,
51 Winchester Avenue, London NW6 7TT
(01–328 0918)

A walk-in service for young people (age 16–23) to discuss their problems.

BRITISH PREGNANCY ADVISORY SERVICE
Head Office, Austy Manor,
Wootton Wawen, Solihull,
West Midlands B95 6DA
(Henley-in-Arden 3225)

A non-profit making charitable trust for pregnancy diagnosis, advice about abortion, and male and female sterilization. Eleven main branches.

CAMPAIGN FOR HOMOSEXUAL EQUALITY (CHE)
P.O. Box 427, 33 King St,
Manchester M60 2EL (061–228 1985)

ERICKSON EDUCATIONAL FOUNDATION
1627 Moreland Ave, Baton Rouge,
La 70808, U.S.A.

For all aspects of transsexualism.

FAMILY DOCTOR PUBLICATIONS
B.M.A. House, Tavistock Square,
London NW1H 9JP (01–387 9721)

Publish a whole range of popular but authoritative booklets on
pregnancy and childbirth, V.D., homosexuality and sex education.

FAMILY PLANNING ASSOCIATION
Margaret Pyke House, 27–35 Mortimer St,
London W1N 7RJ (01–636 7866)

Information bureau. Medical advice and assistance for involuntary sterility, sexual and marital difficulties.

FORUM CLINIC
The Forum Personal Adviser, 2 Bramber Rd,
London W14 9PB (01–385 6181)

Help, information, advice, counselling service and therapy for
sexual and marital problems. Private and confidential. Consultation fee (£0.50) payable in advance. Write for appointment.

GAY CHRISTIAN MOVEMENT
c/o The Gable, Mount Pleasant,
Cambridge.

GAY SWITCHBOARD
01–837 7324

London based, 24 hour telephone service for homosexuals.

London Youth Advisory Service
Camden Branch, 26 Prince of Wales Road,
London NW5 (01–267 4792)

A confidential advice and counselling service for young people
(aged 13–25). A small fee may be charged.

Mind (National Association for Mental Health)
22 Harley St, London W1N 2ED
(01–637 0741)

Social work department offers free advice on most nervous
and psychiatric problems. Many useful publications on mental
health topics from MIND/NAMH Bookshop, 157 Woodhouse
Lane, Leeds LS2 3EF (0532–453926)

The National Marriage Guidance Council
Herbert Gray College, Little Church Street,
Rugby, Warwicks CV21 3AP
(0788–73241)

Are in the process of organizing regional sex therapy clinics.
Already provide a counselling service for marital and psycho-
sexual difficulties. Appointments through local offices. No fee.
Many useful publications.

Parents Enquiry
16 Honley Road, Catford,
London SE6 2HZ (01–698–1815)

For parents of homosexuals and young homosexuals (aged
14–19).

Rape Crisis Centre
P.O. Box 42, London N6 5BU
(01–340 6913)

Provides emotional support, legal and medical advice for women
and children who have been raped or sexually assaulted.
(01–340 6145) For emergency help and advice on all aspects of
rape.

PHYLLIS WRIGHT (HEALTH AND HYGIENE) LTD
34 St George's Walk
Croydon CR0 1YJ
(01–681 1298)

Specialists in marital sexual aids. Confidential service for adults; personal and mail order.